Jungle Nurse

COMPILED BY

Peggy Burton

Publishers :

King's Highway Books
P.O. Box 789
Sutton Coldfield
West Midlands
B73 5FX
ENGLAND

Publishers :
King's Highway Books
P.O. Box 789
Sutton Coldfield
West Midlands
B73 5FX
ENGLAND

Further information or more copies can be obtained from :
Miss Mary Hitchings
110 Downland Avenue
Southwick
West Sussex
BN42 4RY
ENGLAND

ISBN 0-9541015-6-1

All profits from the sale of Jungle Nurse will be donated to Holland Road Baptist Church's new building project.

Printed by : Selsey Press Ltd, 84 High Street, Selsey, Chichester, West Sussex PO20 0QH Tel:01243 605234

Contents

Acknowledgements

First of all I will always be so grateful to my Father, who saved every letter which I sent home from Congo, thus enabling this book to be written. In his lifetime it was always his wish I write this book.

Also to the Baptist Missionary Society World Mission for the wonderful loving way in which they supported their missionaries, and for all their continuing concern and care for us during our retirement years.

I would like to thank Holland Road Baptist Church, Hove, for all their love and prayerful care and support for me over the years, and still do.

I am also grateful to Morden Baptist Church in Surrey, who provided an electric generator, which enabled us to have a good light when operating in the theatre at night in Tondo, without having to rely on hurricane lamps and torches.

I cannot thank Dr James and Peggy Burton enough, who have worked with me at Tondo, for all their hard work which has made the editing of this book possible.

I do thank all my friends and relations who have faithfully supported me over the years – thank you, everyone.

I thank God most of all for the health and strength that He has given me, and for His promise which He gave me so long ago.

'Faithful is He that calleth you, who also will do it.'

1 Thessalonians 5v24

All praise and glory to God.

Mary Hitchings.

Foreword

I first met Mary Hitchings, who features in this book, at Tondo in the Democratic Republic of Congo. The 50 bed hospital there kept us busy but we enjoyed working together. There was also the busy Out Patients Department.

Very unexpectedly, a cable arrived for me one day, saying that I must return home immediately, because of serious family illness.

Mary was therefore left on her own along with the African nurses. She rose to the situation admirably, coping with the language, and whether or not the times were difficult or indeed dangerous, continued to serve the people of Tondo and the surrounding area for some 30 years. (1954-1984)

I count it a real joy and privilege to have been asked to write this Foreword. Mary has meant so much to me, and to many others over the years, both in Congo and in this country, and I know that in all the years that may lie ahead, our friendship will remain strong and meaningful.

Miss F.P.M. Russell. (Patsy)

———————

Preface

Mary really wrote this book and it is just my privilege to sort it all out for her. My husband, James, also had a lot to say, remembering the time Mary arrived at Tondo while we were still there. She worked with him in the hospital, so he is able to explain some of the activities that she mentions.

I have made an effort to thread both their thoughts together with my own thoughts, and thus hope to create a story that will be a source of information and interest for the reader.

It must be understood that Congo is very different today, and many incidents mentioned in this book may not be the same now. Missionaries tend to go out more on short term service rather than periods of up to 30 years.

———————

Mary Hitchings

Chapter 1

CALAMITY!

He brought me up also out of an horrible pit, out of the miry clay,
and set my feet upon a rock, and established my goings.
Psalm 40v2 (A.V.)

It was a beautiful evening with a gentle breeze, and birds singing in the tall palm trees. 'I'm going to be so happy here,' thought Mary as she wandered through the little garden at the back of her new Congo home. Then suddenly, without warning, the ground under her feet gave way.

"Oh!" she cried as she descended into the depths beneath. "What is happening?"

This all happened the day after Mary moved into the new nurses' house that had recently been built. No one had thought to block off the old outside toilet however, and as Mary was wandering around examining the fences and thinking how she could develop the garden, she happened to step on top of the old structure which was now overgrown and hidden in the undergrowth.

Without further ado, Mary landed on the floor of the pit with a resounding plop! A sea of creepy crawlies scattered in all directions to escape the sudden invasion that had disturbed their peaceful abode. 'Oh dear,' she thought, 'How am I going to get out of this?'

She could just touch the top of the pit with the tips of her fingers, but when she tried to make foot holes in the cavity sides, the soil just crumbled.

'How will I make my presence known, or do I stay here all night?' she thought, as evening was quickly approaching. 'I wonder, if I remove my white waist slip and fix it to this stick, I might just be able to wave it above the pit and hope that someone will see it.' So the thought was put into action; slip removed, attached to the stick and raised. It was just long enough to wave. Then at the top of her voice she yelled. "Yaka, yaka, sunga ngai." (Come and help me) Then it was just a matter of waiting and praying!

It so happened that the Congolese nurse on duty at the hospital that evening, needed Mary's help and advice about a seriously ill child that had just arrived, so he decided to see if she was in her home and would come to the hospital.

'Where is she?' thought Nkumu as he knocked on the door and received no reply. 'I wonder where she has gone?' (Mama ajali wapi?)

He wandered round to the back of the house and glanced across the garden. There was no sign of her. Then suddenly, he stopped and his glance became a gaze..

'Mo!' he cried, thrusting his hand over his mouth. (a Congolese sign of surprise) 'What is that white thing I can see wafting in the breeze? There is a muffled sound coming from that direction too. I must go and find out.' So began the start of a serious investigation!

'I don't believe it.' muttered Nkumu to himself. That white thing is moving. What is it doing here in the middle of Mama's garden?' As he came nearer to the 'mystery' he noticed that the ground was disturbed. Then he saw the hole. Yes, the 'white thing' was coming out of the hole and it was definitely moving!

"Who is down there?" he called.

"Ngai (me) Nkumu. I'm so glad you have come." said Mary. "I slipped and fell and can't get out. No one told me there was a hole in my garden."

"Mama! Oh how terrible! What to do?"

"Go For help. Find a ladder; quick, Nkumu. Call Pastor Ngando. Get me out of here. Lots of insects; I'm being eaten alive!" she cried.

"Hold on, Mama, I go; I come back noki noki (quick, quick)" With these parting words Nkumu dashed off and made his way to find Pastor Ngando.

"Have you got a ladder, Pastor? There is an emergency; I need a ladder."

"What ever is the matter, Nkumu. Have you gone mad? Why are you leaping around like that and what do want a ladder in the hospital for, may I ask?"

2

"Can't explain now," said Nkumu. "Just come with me and bring a ladder. I'll explain later. Mama is down a hole and is being eaten alive!"

"What! Eaten alive? Where is she to be in such a state?" puffed Pastor Ngando as he tried to keep up with Nkumu.

It did not take long for the news to get around, and by the time the ladder had been procured and the two men had run back to Mary's house, half the village was aware of Mary's predicament and made haste to join the growing crowd of sight-seers. The children of course, thought it was great fun! Arriving at the scene, the ladder was quickly lowered.

"Thank goodness you've arrived." Cried Mary in a mixture of English and Lingala. "I'll be so glad to get out of here."

As Mary slowly ascended the ladder, the two men grasped her hand and with loud cheers from the gathering crowds, she slowly emerged into the fading daylight, somewhat grubby but apparently unharmed.

"We must get that hole filled in before I come this way again." She said. "I can think of better places to spend a quiet hour." She said to nobody in particular!

"Go and have a bath, Mama." Explained Pastor Ngando, "before you go to the hospital to see the sick child that has just arrived. They need your help and advice, so don't be long."

So this was the experience Mary had as she took up residence in the new nurses' house; a day she will not forget in a hurry.

———————————

Chapter 2

HOW IT ALL BEGAN

I will instruct you and teach you in the way you should go; I will
counsel you and watch over you.
Psalm 32v8 (NIV)

Mary was just fifteen years old when, one Sunday morning she was
sitting in church – and feeling rather bored! In the pew in front of her
at Florence Road Baptist Church, Brighton, was a pamphlet, which she
idly picked up to read. It was a pamphlet from the Baptist Missionary
Society. As she held it in her hand she was very conscious that it was as
if God was talking to her – 'One day you will be a missionary with the
BMS.'- She did not actually hear a voice, but never the less she felt that
this was what He was saying. There and then she told God that He had
made a mistake. She was not the sort of person He could use on the
mission field. She did not share this experience with anyone but, like
Mary of old, 'kept and pondered it in her heart.'

After leaving school and secretarial training, she worked in the office
of an Estate Agent, then in1942 she was called up during the time of the
Second World War, to work in a nuts and bolts factory at Maidenhead.
During this time she still attended church and had many Christian
friends, but still did not respond to God's call, that had come to her
during those earlier years. Deep inside however, there was an awareness
that she was not really in the right place.

Later, because of the need for a minor operation, she had to attend
Maidenhead General Hospital. As she watched the nurses working, she
somehow knew in her heart that she too, should be working
somewhere, helping other people. 'These nurses really are helping
people,' she thought. 'Maybe I should be doing something like that; I
wonder!' But still the idea of missionary work did not come to mind.
God was speaking again and this time Mary took more notice.

To change one's job during war time however, meant that there were
only a few options; the Land Army, the Armed Forces or Nursing. 'That's
it!' thought Mary. 'Nursing.' So she immediately sent an application for

nursing training, to the Matron of the Kent and Sussex Hospital in Tunbridge Wells.

One morning, soon after, she received two official looking letters. One was from her former employer notifying her that the Armed Forces were requisitioning all the hotels on the Brighton and Hove sea front and that, with permission from the War Office, she was called back to work with them. The other letter was from the Matron at Tunbridge Wells to say that she had been accepted to train as a probationary nurse as requested, and should report to the hospital in September 1944.

So Mary began her nursing training and unbeknown to her at the time, God was preparing her for the future. General training was followed by midwifery and district nursing; they were such happy years. At the same time she was drawing closer to God, culminating in a final response to the call she had first heard and rejected so many years before.   Mary was now in membership at Holland Road Baptist Church in Hove. During the yearly Missionary week it was the churches' custom to hold a special 'Young Peoples' Meeting.' It was at this meeting that a special challenge of commitment to full time service overseas would be given. Mary was doubtful about going to this particular meeting and she prayed for a definite sign that this really was for her. She would not go to the meeting without knowing that this was the right thing to do. Nothing happened, so she just told God that she would not go to the meeting. Then, about 7pm the Nursing Superintendent called, asking Mary to attend an emergency case. This was a good excuse not to go to the meeting! But God had His plans, and as Mary entered the bedroom of the 'emergency case,' she was immediately confronted by a text above the bed.

'Faithful is He who calleth thee, who also will do it.'
2 Thessalonians 5v24

This is all she needed to know! When her duty was complete she returned to the Nurses' Home, then went straight to the church to attend the meeting which, by this time, was nearly over. But she was just in time to hear Pastor Rudman saying,

"If there is any young person here called to the mission field, will they come on to the platform and shake my hand."

Mary walked straight down the aisle and on to the platform before she even sat down! She shook his hand with joy in her heart.

A long spell of training and preparation followed this vital decision before Mary was equipped for the way ahead. She felt that the B.M.S. was not the right missionary society for her, so wrote to another mission. But after considerable thoughts and doubts, she did finally offer to the Baptist Missionary Society, conscious that God was calling her to witness and nurse amongst the people of the Equatorial Province of Congo. On acceptance, a time of Bible training was followed by further preparation in Brussels and Antwerp in Belgium, in order to qualify for work in the Congo.

The year was 1954 and she was warmly welcomed by the Baptist Missionary Society at this particular time. Two nursing sisters at the lakeside station of Tondo had to return to the UK for health reasons; Patsy Russell and Pauline Trounson. Together they had been supervising the hospital programme and their departure would result in serious problems if there was no replacement for the hospital. Mary's availability was a wonderful answer to the prayers of many people.

Thus began the busiest three weeks that Mary had ever experienced. Shopping for necessary items, packing, with the very difficult task of keeping the weight to only 20 kilos of luggage for the flight. Then there was the farewell to friends and family and a wonderful valedictory service at the church. Finally, all was complete and by October 1954 Mary was ready to launch out into the biggest adventure of her life.

The check-in desk at the airport revealed what she did not wish to hear.

"Your luggage is very much overweight, Madam." stated the lady at the desk.

"Oh!" Mary said. "Now what shall I do?"

The desk lady then looked at her and said in a low voice, "Only mercenaries or missionaries go to a country like Congo." It didn't really bother Mary which category she was placed in; she was just very relieved that she had nothing extra to pay! The Lord indeed, looks after His own.

Final farewells, and then through the barrier and on to the plane. Soon up to 35,000 feet and just a black speck visible to the family watching from the look-out area at the airport. There was no turning back now for Mary; she was on her way, leaving family and friends and everything she loved, heading into a completely unknown future.

But when we obey God's calling for our lives and are prepared to go where He chooses to send us, we have the assurance of knowing that our Lord and Saviour will always be with us. This is how Mary faced the future; she had been particularly encouraged by a passage of Scripture that Pastor Rudman from Holland Road Baptist Church had given her as she left.

'If I take the wings of the morning, and dwell in the uttermost parts of the sea; even there shall Thy hand lead me, and Thy right hand shall hold me.' (Psalm 139v9-10)

Thus Mary had embarked on the first stage of a new life-style; a ministry of love and concern for a needy world, ready to play her part in the place of God's appointment, knowing that He would not expect her to do more than He would give her the ability to do.

Chapter 3

PASTURES NEW

Therefore go and make disciples of all nations.
Matthew 28v19(NIV)

Arriving at Tondo

As the 'plane droned on, Mary was lulled into a comforting feeling of relaxation. The previous weeks had not been easy with so much to do, plus farewells with family and friends. Until now, she had not realised how tired she really was. Then, as she casually gazed out of the window, she suddenly sat up.

'Ah! I can see the coast of Africa,' she said to herself. 'Wonderful! I'm almost there!' Then as the aircraft slowly descended, she could see the airport, and very soon it was time to step out on to African soil. Mary's future was about to begin.

Only those who have experienced their first faltering steps in the land of God's choosing for their ministry, can appreciate how Mary felt at this point. Thrilling anticipation thrilled her heart. How many missionaries before her had experienced this unexplainable event.

The first thing that hit Mary was the heat, but at the same time it struck her how unexpectedly clean and organised everything was here in the middle of Africa! She soon completed the necessary formalities, then was greeted by a group of friendly faces holding a large BMS placard.

"Welcome to Congo." They called to her.

"I'm so glad to be here at last." she replied. "It has been a long journey, but oh! It is so good to be here, even if I feel the heat. I expect I'll soon get used to it."

This joyful meeting was followed by a 32 kilometre drive to the BMS compound in Kinshasa. Mary noticed everything so different as they advanced along the rough road; a lack of greenery and the scenery tinted with a shade of brown. Even the atmosphere smelt different. She was fascinated by the people; lots of people, chattering loudly as they went.

"The people don't seem to be wearing any shoes." Mary remarked in surprise.

"Oh, that is normal. They seem to have feet like iron; it doesn't seem to worry them."

"How do those women manage to cope with a baby on their backs and at the same time balance such a load on their heads?" asked Mary.

"They get used to it," said Andrew, the driver. "After all, it is their job to do the carrying, and at the same time, it is their job to take care of the children. They can't leave the baby on its own, so when they have to get the firewood or anything else, they have to take the baby with them. The only way is to fix them on to their backs; it seems to work." There were no baby buggies in Congo at that time.

So Mary's trip through the city streets of Kinshasa proved to be quite an experience. There was shopping to be done for herself and items requested from Tondo, the station to which she would be going. Necessary paper work had to be completed too. The Belgian authorities would not allow any medical workers to practice in the Province without official permission. On top of all these commitments there were the complications of dealing in a different coinage, and strange languages to decipher apart from French. It was not an easy time for Mary as she prepared to travel up into the interior.

The time came for her to move back to the airport. This time to board a smaller 'plane, then a fascinating flight of some 1,120 kilometres north. They flew low enough for Mary to look down over the great

Congo River winding its way through the vast forested area of the Congo Basin. She was even able to pick out a herd of elephants in one of the forest clearings. What an amazing experience this was at the very start of a new life into an unknown future, but she was conscious of God's presence guiding and directing her all the way.

Back to earth again, literally, and through the formalities at Mbandaka airport, then to be greeted by Dr James Burton, with whom she would be working in the hospital at Tondo.

"Mary, it is lovely to welcome you," he said, with a large welcoming smile. "Have you had a good flight? The car is just outside, so we will make a start when you are ready. Have you checked your luggage?" Thus through the clatter and chatter of bustling Africans, they made their way out of the airport, into the car and away.

"We'll stop at an American Mission station just outside the city," said James. "They are our nearest neighbours, 136 kilometres away, and are always so helpful and kind to us. They will give us some lunch before we get on the road for Tondo."

"Thank you, that will be lovely," said Mary. "I'm quite ready for something; we didn't have much on the 'plane, but I was too fascinated by all I saw out of the window, including my first sight of a herd of elephants!" she exclaimed. "The forest just went on and on. I've never seen so many trees. How far does it go?"

"I think it covers over 4000 kilometres all together," replied James as he narrowly missed a stray goat that bounced unexpectedly across the road. "It goes right up to the east of Congo, bordering on to Ruanda Urundi, where the land is much higher."

"May I introduce you to Miss Mary Hitchings, who is coming to Tondo to help us in the hospital." James said to Steve, when they arrived at the mission station of the Disciples of Christ Mission.

"Pleased to meet you, Mary," said Steve. "Don't let them work you too hard. You know what these English missionaries are like!!"

"Oh, don't worry, Steve," said James. "We are so glad that she has been able to come; a real answer to our prayers. We will look after her alright. Now that Patsy Russell and Pauline Trounson have had to return home, Mary will be very warmly welcomed." 'I only hope I'm up to all their expectations,' thought Mary.

After meeting some of the missionaries over lunch, James and Mary proceeded on their way, but they could not hurry on the rough, stony road, intercepted by so many insecure wooden bridges. On journeys through the Congo forest in those days, it was not unusual to come upon ruts and potholes and mud, and often it was necessary to stop and put leaves and branches under the wheels of the car to get mobile again. This would be a distinct possibility during the rainy season.

There were many little bridges made of round poles that lay over small streams or dykes along the Congo roads, and these were constantly being attacked by termites or borers, thus weakening the poles and causing them to give way under a heavy vehicle. It was always advisable to stop and test a bridge by jumping on it! All this took time, but James did not want to drop Mary in the river before she had even arrived at Tondo! When a road surface did appear to be reasonably flat, so that they could make some headway, it was not unusual for a pack of monkeys to suddenly appear and dash across the road in front of them.

Mary took it all in. "My, this is an exciting journey," she exclaimed. "I will never forget my introduction to Congo and all the unusual things that are happening. Can you imagine monkeys doing that at home, unless you are in somewhere like Longleat."

"Yes, you never know what you are going to encounter on these forest tracks," said James, carefully avoiding a large anthill in the middle of the road. "One day I drove over an enormous snake; a boa constrictor, I think. It's head was in the forest on one side of the road and it's tail was in the forest on the other side of the road. I though it was a tree until I saw it moving!"

As they got nearer to Tondo, they passed through many villages.

"Why are so many people lining the sides of the road?" asked Mary. "They look so friendly, and just look at the little children." "This is all for your benefit," replied James. They heard that you were coming to join us at Tondo and they are out to welcome you. The message to say that we are on our way will have been passed on from village to village over the drum language. We don't have phones or other ways of passing on messages out here, you know. By the time we reach the mission,

Welcome

everyone will be there to greet you because the drum message will have told them where we are and that we will soon be arriving."

"That's amazing," said Mary. "I'm so excited."

So it was that as they neared the station more and more people seemed to appear from nowhere, all cheering and waving as the travellers passed. Mary just gasped; she could hardly believe this was happening.

"Even the Queen could not have a more enthusiastic welcome than this," she remarked.

Then they arrived at the Mission entrance. Now the road was lined with school children, looking very smart in their neat blue uniforms. They too, were waving and singing a song of welcome. Slowly the car came to a halt and Mary emerged amidst cheers from the growing crowd. Pastor Ngando Pierre, the senior Congolese Pastor came forward first, then Ikoma Denis, the Congolese head nurse at the hospital. Next Mongu Raymond, the Congolese senior school teacher. Finally, welcomes and greetings from Peggy Burton with daughters Josephine aged 5 and Rosemary aged 3. Lyn Collis, the builder, with Joan his wife and daughter Juliet aged 8. Winifred Hadden, Headmistress of the school and Sylvia Varley who had come to work with Mary from another station, for a three month period.

So amidst all the excitement Mary was then taken to Winifred Hadden's house with whom she was to make her home. A welcome cup of tea was waiting for her before a conducted tour of the house completed the activities of the day. What a lot had happened since she had said her farewells back in England. That time seemed so far away now; so many new experiences, but there were still many more to come.

———————

Chapter 1

CALAMITY!

*He brought me up also out of an horrible pit, out of the miry clay,
and set my feet upon a rock, and established my goings.*
Psalm 40v2 (A.V.)

It was a beautiful evening with a gentle breeze, and birds singing in the tall palm trees. 'I'm going to be so happy here,' thought Mary as she wandered through the little garden at the back of her new Congo home. Then suddenly, without warning, the ground under her feet gave way.

"Oh!" she cried as she descended into the depths beneath. "What is happening?"

This all happened the day after Mary moved into the new nurses' house that had recently been built. No one had thought to block off the old outside toilet however, and as Mary was wandering around examining the fences and thinking how she could develop the garden, she happened to step on top of the old structure which was now overgrown and hidden in the undergrowth.

Without further ado, Mary landed on the floor of the pit with a resounding plop! A sea of creepy crawlies scattered in all directions to escape the sudden invasion that had disturbed their peaceful abode. 'Oh dear,' she thought, 'How am I going to get out of this?'

She could just touch the top of the pit with the tips of her fingers, but when she tried to make foot holes in the cavity sides, the soil just crumbled.

'How will I make my presence known, or do I stay here all night?' she thought, as evening was quickly approaching. 'I wonder, if I remove my white waist slip and fix it to this stick, I might just be able to wave it above the pit and hope that someone will see it.' So the thought was put into action; slip removed, attached to the stick and raised. It was just long enough to wave. Then at the top of her voice she yelled. "Yaka, yaka, sunga ngai." (Come and help me) Then it was just a matter of waiting and praying!

It so happened that the Congolese nurse on duty at the hospital that evening, needed Mary's help and advice about a seriously ill child that had just arrived, so he decided to see if she was in her home and would come to the hospital.

'Where is she?' thought Nkumu as he knocked on the door and received no reply. 'I wonder where she has gone?' (Mama ajali wapi?)

He wandered round to the back of the house and glanced across the garden. There was no sign of her. Then suddenly, he stopped and his glance became a gaze..

'Mo!' he cried, thrusting his hand over his mouth. (a Congolese sign of surprise) 'What is that white thing I can see wafting in the breeze? There is a muffled sound coming from that direction too. I must go and find out.' So began the start of a serious investigation!

'I don't believe it.' muttered Nkumu to himself. That white thing is moving. What is it doing here in the middle of Mama's garden?' As he came nearer to the 'mystery' he noticed that the ground was disturbed. Then he saw the hole. Yes, the 'white thing' was coming out of the hole and it was definitely moving!

"Who is down there?" he called.

"Ngai (me) Nkumu. I'm so glad you have come." said Mary. "I slipped and fell and can't get out. No one told me there was a hole in my garden."

"Mama! Oh how terrible! What to do?"

"Go For help. Find a ladder; quick, Nkumu. Call Pastor Ngando. Get me out of here. Lots of insects; I'm being eaten alive!" she cried. "Hold on, Mama, I go; I come back noki noki (quick, quick)" With these parting words Nkumu dashed off and made his way to find Pastor Ngando.

"Have you got a ladder, Pastor? There is an emergency; I need a ladder."

"What ever is the matter, Nkumu. Have you gone mad? Why are you leaping around like that and what do want a ladder in the hospital for, may I ask?"

this little church. But before we leave, let me introduce you to one of our oldest patients."

They walked over to one of the little huts.

"Nsomboli," called out James "Mbote Mama. Yaka awa." (Greetings, Mama. Come here.)

Then from the dark interior, blinking against the bright sunshine, emerged a little old lady, crippled and disfigured by the ravages of leprosy, which, in the past, had not been treated. But she was radiantly smiling as James introduced her to Mary.

"I have brought our new nurse to greet you," said James.

"Mbote, Mama."(greetings, Mama) Nsomboli said to Mary.

"Disfigured she may be," said James, "But Nsomboli is one of the most radiant Christians in the Centre. She came to us some time ago, rejected by her own people, but has found here a living faith. It is always a great joy to take communion with her, realising we are all 'one in Christ Jesus.' "

Mary was silent as she walked back with James to the main hospital compound, where crowds had already increased. Would she ever be able to cope with the tasks ahead to which God had called her? In her own strength, 'No' but God had given her the promise 'Faithful is He who calleth you, who will do it.'

So ended the tour; now for the real thing.

Chapter 5

FIRST IMPRESSIONS

Therefore if any man be in Christ, he is a new creature: old things are
passed away;
behold all things are become new.
2Corinthians 5v17 (AV)

Batwa children

A new country, new culture, new language, new colleagues and new
name. There was so much for Mary to take in and understand during
her first months at Tondo. Without a knowledge of the language, it
would be impossible to communicate with the Congolese, unless they
spoke French, as some of them did, apart from the village folk. This all
meant that for a start, language study was a priority.

However, overall, Mary's first impressions encouraged her. The
hospital, school and church seemed to be well managed and everyone
was so friendly. She was especially impressed by the beauty of the Tondo
gardens and the surrounding countryside. The dense forest, tall
coconut palms and the beautiful lake, with gently lapping water on to
the sandy beach. She was fascinated by the lakeside village and the
happy little children playing there. Then there were the chickens, ducks
and goats wandering freely everywhere, and a host of beautiful birds

singing and flying around, to bring a delightful sense of well being to her wandering thoughts. It was all so much to take in.

Then she thought of the many needs there were here amongst the people; medical and spiritual. This gave her a positive sense of assurance, that she was indeed in the place that God had already planned for her so many years ago. She felt so certain, and this gave her a wonderful feeling of satisfaction and joy.   As her thoughts continued to wander during those first dramatic months, she considered so many things that were new experiences for her. Housekeeping for a start, was very different, but as Winnie slowly introduced her to various aspects in this department, she gradually came to terms with all the different methods. With no refrigerator, food had to be kept in a gauze fitted larder on the balcony, the legs of which had to be kept in tins of paraffin to prevent the little red ants from entering. The tins had to be checked each day to remove any little 'cobwebs' that would provide an excellent 'bridge' for the ants!

The main diet was fish from the lake and chicken or duck that was kept on the station. Meat was scarce for the simple reason there was nothing very suitable apart from antelope or goat. You could of course, always have a go at snake cutlets, stewed monkey, elephant steaks, porcupine, fried crocodile, wild boar, fat caterpillars, locusts, rats or bats. These were all to be found on the African menu! There was always of course, plenty of fruit and vegetables grown on the station; pai-pai (Paw-paw) plantain, bananas, citrus fruits, guavas and mangos. Tinned goods and groceries in general, had to be ordered from the UK or bought at Mbandaka 136 kilometres away.

Probably one of the most difficult things to get acclimatised to, were the insects. Large, shiny mahogany brown cockroaches with long, twitching antennae, that scurried about at alarming speeds, or congregated in cupboards and dark corners. They ate paint off the picture frames and furniture and they chewed the book covers. Mary had to get used to fixing a mosquito net over her bed each night, not only to protect her from the mosquito, but it also kept out other insects and pests.   There were so many other insects that she would meet as time went on. Driver ants, termites, elephant flies, mason wasps, millipedes and scorpions, to name just a few. All contributed to a host of new experiences for Mary.

So slowly she began to fit into a new way of life in the heart of the African jungle; it was a very new experience for her. But she was here at the command of her Lord and Master, who had no other plan to spread the Good News of the love of God through salvation, other than relying on His leading.

It is true that missionary work can be so easily glamorised, but serving suffering humanity is not a romantic event, especially in such primitive conditions. Mary was beginning to realise this and through it all, she was beginning to learn. Much more lay ahead and she would accept each event in due course, knowing that the Lord would enable her to do so.

Chapter 6

INTRODUCTION TO A
JUNGLE HOSPITAL

And He sent them out to preach the Kingdom of God,
and to heal the sick.
Luke 9v2 (AV)

"I am enjoying Congo breakfasts," said Mary, as Winnie handed her half
an enormous paw-paw. "Bembe picked it this morning," replied Winnie.
"That tree I pointed out to you yesterday has done so well this year. I
never get tired of paw-paw. You will miss them when you go home."

"That won't be yet, Winnie, I've only just got here! Oh no! Look at the
time. I must get moving. James wants to take me round the wards this
morning, to introduce me to some of the patients and point out some of
the illnesses we have to deal with here. I expect they seem very different
to the ones I am used to." With that Mary made her way towards the
hospital along the cliff path overlooking the lake. She was anxious to
get to grips with yet another experience.

The hospital had no gas, electricity, running water or plumbing, so
— —'s first impressions had been 'How could she maintain the
standard of nursing that she had known at home?' A small laboratory,
a microscope and an operating table made a start, but sterilization of
theatre linen etc, had to be done in sterilizers balanced on a camp fire in
the open hospital 'kitchen' area! – No pre - packed sterile system in those
days.

"Good morning, Mary." James called out to her as she made her way
through the crowds gathering for morning prayers. "I trust you are
refreshed after a relaxing night." She did not let on about the rats and
the drums! "Let me introduce you to Nsomo, our hospital evangelist,"
he continued as a broad, smiling faced African approached them. He
was calling the people together and attempting to sort out various
arguments.

"Mbote,(greetings) Mama," he said, as he grasped her hand enthusiastically and stumbled over a stray chicken that decided to join the mayhem.

By this time Mary was quite overcome by the volume of people trying to pack into an inadequate sized 'waiting room.' Nsomo continued his shepherding, collecting folks from all around the hospital; mobile patients from the wards together with their relatives and helpers from the cook house. Soon the crowds filled the hospital compound completely and the service began.

Ikoma - Head Nurse

"We usually leave the nurses to sort everyone out at this point," said James to Mary after the service, "while we do a ward round and arrange the programme of the day. Ikoma will come with us and I will introduce you to some of the very interesting cases we have in the hospital at the moment. Many of the patients come with treatable conditions and it is a joy to send them back to their villages fit and healthy. But sadly, some come too late for even modern medicine or surgery to cure. Let's go into the men's ward first."

The ward was crowded with patients, their relatives wandering about, some with the patients' meals followed by the family dog and maybe a child hanging on too.

"This little boy," said James, "is about 10 years old. He came in with a grossly swollen abdomen and pathetically thin arms and legs. He was also suffering from severe malnutrition and was very anaemic from chronic malaria. On investigation, we found that he was full of intestinal parasites; hook worm, that drains the blood system."

Mary had studied the effects of this common worm in her tropical medicine lectures, but had never seen the devastating effects of such massive parasite infestation in a child.

"We'll deal with his problems one by one," James said, "and hope to send him back to his village cured and happy as the children should be. We try to encourage the building of proper latrines in the villages, to create proper sanitation, which will prevent these children from picking up the hook worm larvae."

They moved on to another patient. "This man had multiple fractures when he fell from a huge palm tree. He was cutting a bunch of palm nuts and he slipped. We've patched him up, but without the benefit of x-rays to help, it was not easy. We hope he will stay long enough to enable his fractures to heal. Sometimes we have a problem," James chuckled. "One man who had a similar fall, was so anxious to return to his village. The relatives too, were not keen for him to stay with us. I knew there was likely to be trouble so I put on a really hefty plaster. Sure enough, he disappeared during the night; we often wonder how they eventually got the plaster off his leg back in the village!"

Mary smiled as she thought of this man tramping through the forest with that plaster securely attached to his leg!

So they went from bed to bed, examining the patients and writing up treatments for a wide variety of medical and surgical problems. 'How will I remember everything?' thought Mary.

"Let's go across to the women's ward," said James. Again there was a hive of activity going on and every bed was full. First of all they went over to see two women with their babies, recovering from recent caesarean section operations.

"Unfortunately, Mary, we have to resort to caesarean deliveries in some cases, as so many mothers have a deformed, flat pelvis, caused by carrying enormous weights of manioc from their forest gardens in big baskets on their backs when they were young. These deformities often lead to difficult child birth in later years."

"Oh!" remarked Mary, "Don't those babies look sweet in those little vests."

"Yes," replied James, "they all come out from England in the 'Wants boxes.' Many people at home knit them and we are so thrilled to receive them. We like to give one to each new baby born in the hospital if we have enough. Nights can be very cold in the forest villages and often the babies are left to lie on the cold, hard mud floors; they need something warm like these little vests."

As they went round the ward they saw one case after another; women recovering from various abdominal operations, others recovering from severe burns etc. All needing as much care as this little hospital could give them.

After the ward rounds, Mary joined Sylvia at the weekly Kilo clinic (baby clinic) while James went to his office. This was a happy occasion with chattering mothers and their little babies in the brightly coloured vests. Each baby was weighed and examined and then the mothers were given a bar of soap.

"These soap bars are one of the attractions of the 'Kilo' clinic," laughed Sylvia. "But it enables us to check up on the babies in the hope that they will keep fit and well back in their little mud village huts. We try to help the Mums to look after and wean their babies, otherwise they tend to stuff them with indigestible manioc at an early age before the child is ready to take it. Sadly, neo-natal mortality is high in the villages."

Clinic over, Mary wandered over to see what was going on in the Out Patients.

"Gracious!" she cried, "What ever is happening in that queue by the pharmacy window?" She went closer and could hardly believe what she was seeing. There was the leading patient in the front of the queue standing there with her mouth wide open and the nurse pouring in medicine! The next one came, with open mouth to receive some pills to be washed down with a cup of water. From his office James saw the look of surprise on Mary's face. He came over.

"Don't look so surprised, Mary. We have to do this, otherwise the medicines would be taken back to the village and sold to the highest bidder as a very strong native medicine from the 'white' doctor!"

So Mary's first morning in the hospital drew to a close and she was glad of the established custom of a break for lunch and a very necessary 'siesta' before the afternoon programme, which would involve any particular treatments, clinics or possibly a visit to a village.

Chapter 7

DAILY MEDICAL CHALLENGES

And whatever you do, whether in word or deed, do it all
in the name of the Lord Jesus,
Giving thanks to God the Father through Him.
Colossians 3v17(NIV)

As Mary later quoted in a report home:

"The hospital at Tondo serves a population of about ten thousand people. Our patients come from the inland villages and those scattered around Lake Tumba . The lake is about 48 kilometres long by 32 kilometres wide. The patients travel by dug out canoes which do not weather rough waters, and sometimes an ill patient cannot be brought into Tondo for two or three days until the lake is calm. This can be disastrous where acutely ill patients are concerned. The whole family together with cooking utensils and food, will have to be brought too. The trip to Tondo, therefore, is very hazardous and many people have been drowned while travelling on the lake. This is another good reason for them to try local native medicine before facing the long journey to Tondo!

People who come from the interior may have to travel from 48 to 80 kilometres or more on very bad roads. They usually come on foot or by bicycle. Often a bicycle is used as an ambulance for a very sick patient!

Bicycle Ambulance

The hospital day starts at 6am as the station drum sounds out, calling the hospital staff to morning prayers before the routine of the day. Outpatients and morning rounds, then the work programme begins as patients are sorted out for treatment."

As the days and weeks passed, Mary settled into the hospital routine and things were easier as she became more familiar with the language. She continues her report.

"We have a good team of Congolese nurses, some trained and some still in training. The Outpatients department is always very busy with about 200 patients seen every day. On taking case histories, no one knows how old they are, but I know the hospital was built in 1924, so I ask the adults how tall they were when the hospital was first built. This gives me some idea of their age!

There is always a hub of activity in the Outpatients department, babies being born in the maternity ward and constant interruptions when an emergency arrives."

So Mary was confronted with a host of new experiences; language, customs and hospital routine. These were all different to anything she had been accustomed to before. Later on, in a newsletter home she wrote:

" If I were to describe an average patient who comes to the hospital, I would say he has a wonderful sense of humour, is very friendly and has implicit faith that you will be able to cure him and his family of all their ills. He will probably be very poor and will not be able to afford the full cost of his treatment, but he will bring with him a few eggs or perhaps a chicken to pay the rest of his hospital fees. He will be dressed very shabbily and his shirt will be more holes than shirt! There were also of course, those such as Pastors, traders and school teachers etc, who would all be more smartly dressed.

The greatest scourges that undermine the health of the Congolese in this area are malaria intestinal worm infection and leprosy. All have a very debilitating effect on the patients, causing anaemia, chest infections and under nourishment. Tuberculosis is becoming a very serious problem too. Treatment has to be given over a long period and many of the patients cannot afford to stay at Tondo as food is expensive to buy. But they do not take their medicines regularly at home; they may even sell them at a good price!   We have a trained Congolese midwife, and we deliver about 250 babies each year in the hospital. There are however, many mothers who have their babies in the villages; sometimes at the cost of the baby's or mother's life.

Epilepsy is common in the Tondo area. Liema was brought in one day. She had had a fit and fell into the fire. One arm was burnt from the arm-pit to the wrist. On her right side she was burnt from the shoulder to the waist. After many weeks the burns healed but she was left with many scars.

George, a lad of 15, who was mentally retarded, had a fit when he was bathing in the lake. It was too late when we arrived and he drowned. But he loved Jesus and we look forward to meeting him one day; then he will be in his right mind. He was such a lovable lad.

Amba was another epileptic case who came to the hospital with a badly burnt foot after falling in the fire due to a fit. Burn cases are frequently brought into the hospital. Many of them are leprosy casualties whose fingers and feet are immune to feeling; the disease has destroyed the nerve endings. So they take hold of cooking pots or walk through smouldering campfires and have no feeling.

Ingeli was very ill with diabetes. He had a high blood pressure and heart failure too. On returning to the village he was given native medicine and subsequently died.

Then there was the child of two years who suffered convulsions in the village. Grandmother put the child's feet into a bowl of boiling water, to drive out the evil spirit, resulting in burns from toes to ankles. After two and a half months in hospital the feet were nearly healed, but she lost most of her toes and had difficulty in walking. Of course, without toes, she could not balance very well. This would be a great handicap when she became adult and had to grow food for her family in her garden several kilometres from Tondo.   Another ten month old baby fell into the fire and was burnt from arm-pit to thighs on one side. The burns healed well but then he caught measles from other children in the hospital. Thankfully, he survived.

When I first arrived at the hospital it was very busy indeed. Major surgery was being performed two days a week and hundreds of outpatients diagnosed and treated. It was impossible for Dr Burton to run the hospital on his own, without European nurses. No one could have imagined how rapidly this situation was to change within only the next few years. Sylvia Varley and I worked very happily together. No news of Pauline being able to return, but news came through that Patsy would soon be able to return. Then the day came when Sylvia had to leave and return to her work at Kimpese, Lower Congo, many kilometres south of Leopoldville. I busily began to spring clean the hospital from top to bottom in preparation for Patsy's return. I was apprehensive however, as we had never met! Now we would be living and working together seven days a week, but we were sisters in Christ and from the beginning worked and lived very happily together. It is not always so, as often Satan can use broken relationships to do much harm on the mission field. Single missionaries need much prayer support"

In 1956 the time came for James and Peggy Burton, with their two little daughters to return to the UK due to Peggy's heart condition. It was not going to be easy in the hospital until another doctor could come to replace James. Little did Mary realise what the future years held in store for her.

Chapter 8

ACCIDENTS, EMERGENCIES AND CREEPY - CRAWLIES

I can do all things through Christ which strengtheneth me.
Philippians 4v13 (AV)

Soon after coming back to Tondo, Patsy had to return to the UK again due to a family emergency. This meant that Mary was now left in charge of the hospital, on her own for a while with the help of the Congolese nurses. She tells about some of the accidents and emergencies that confronted her during this time.

"Ilondo, aged 12 years, came to us with his father from the village of Mpangi. He had a very badly ulcerated foot which had been treated by the village nurse for about two weeks. When he came to Tondo hospital, the whole of the top of his foot had ulcerated away and the bones were exposed. Pus was copious and flesh was sloughing away. The boy was very anaemic , loosing weight and very frightened. What could we do for him in a bush hospital with no doctor? We treated him with antibiotics and daily dressings, together with treatment for malaria, worm infection and malnutrition. We tried to take his mind off his foot. Eventually we sent him to Mbandaka where there was a doctor. He had two operations followed by a skin graft. After 3 months he returned to Tondo walking normally with a healed foot. I was presented with a chicken; a gift to show their appreciation! He then returned to his village, a normal schoolboy, able to play football and climb trees, but I am sure he will never forget this experience and I hope he will thank God for all the care He took of him.

On another occasion, Boika and Nkumu 'borrowed' their father's bicycle. Well, ' boys will be boys'! Riding through the village with friends, three of them somehow balanced on the bike. Boika, aged 8 years, was at the back and he caught his foot in the wheel. This happened in the village of Mpaha, a few kilometres from Tondo.

Boika's father was angry and he rushed his son to the hospital. We found the big toe nearly off and took about an hour to sew it back on. Fortunately, it healed perfectly with no infection. Boika will not borrow his father's bicycle again in a hurry!

Monzoi was a fisherman. One day he ventured too near to an island in the middle of the lake, and saw what he thought was a log which turned out to be a crocodile. Monzoi was attacked, but miraculously he managed to escape from its jaws, fled up the beach and collapsed. Fortunately, the islanders, who were distant relatives of his, found him and were horrified when they saw the extent of his wounds. They immediately put him on a rough stretcher and paddled him in a canoe across the lake to Tondo. He had five gaping wounds which the relatives had filled with cow dung. This probably saved his life as at least it stemmed the flow of blood from the wounds! It took us four hours to clean and stitch the wounds but, with the help of antibiotics, good nursing by our Congolese nurses and of course, constant prayer, the wounds eventually healed. We also rejoiced that he responded to the message of Jesus and became a vibrant Christian, proclaiming what wonderous things the Lord had done for him."

Everyone living and working in the tropics gets acquainted with the variety of livestock; creepy crawlies, birds and beasts. Mary was no exception, and here she explains some of her observations and experiences. She continues:

"I have often been asked, 'Did you have any snakes at Tondo?' The answer is 'Yes, I did see them from time to time, but it was not a daily occurrence.' Most of them gave a nasty bite but on the whole, were not life threatening. There were a few however, whose bite was poisonous, so every snake was treated as if it could be a killer. We had a 'snake drill' which was used throughout the village. If you were confronted by a snake you shouted as loud as you could, 'Nyoka, nyoka!' (snake, snake) and then folks would rush to your aid with machetes and sticks. Nine times out of ten the snake would be killed. The Batwa folk loved eating snakes but I never tried one!

One memorable day we did have a serious incident. When retiring to bed one night, Arnold and Marjorie Page found a huge python curled up round the leg of their bed. As they entered the bedroom it raised it's ugly head and started hissing. 'Nyoka, nyoka!' they cried. A group of men who had heard their cries, together with Arnold, attacked and killed the offending python. We were all shaken by that event and knew that our Lord had marvellously protected us. We were however, concerned that a mate of the python might be lurking around too, but no sign of it was ever seen.

We did have a Batwa man, Iyanda, come into the hospital one day with a snake bite. His relatives did not think it was a particularly dangerous snake but Iyanda was very frightened. We gave him anti-snake bite injection and a sedative to quieten him, but he died in the night. We did not think he died from the actual snake bite but from the sheer fear of it.

When we were swimming in the lake we were always watchful for water snakes which could give a nasty bite, but if one kept quite still, they would just disappear. However, children would often panic and as a result were occasionally bitten. But to my knowledge, we did not have any more deaths from snake bites.

A hunter, brought into the hospital said he had been mauled by a hippopotamus, but we think it was a buffalo. – At the time, it was illegal to hunt buffalo! – His legs were badly ripped and also there was a long gash in his right arm. To this day he still insists that it was a hippo and not a buffalo! We did have a hippo that came to Tondo beach about 5pm every day. One day my houseboy came rushing into our house. He was a bit late for work because he had overstayed his time at the beach and a hippo chased him from the water. He was very frightened but unharmed. However, we had to send him home that evening as he was not in a fit state to work!"

Creepy crawlies cover a wide range of insects. Mary mentions a few here, that played a part in her Congo experience.

"Large black scorpions have viscous tails with an equally viscous sting, capable of injecting toxins through the skin of anyone with whom it comes into contact. To receive such a sting causes pain like a red hot poker. It was something to be avoided.Before putting on boots, we always had to shake them upside down to make sure no 'nasties' were lurking there. One morning my houseboy, on his way to work, was bitten by a scorpion on his foot and spent the rest of the morning with his foot soaking in a bowl of permanganate of potash, after having received an injection of adrenalin.

Spiders were in abundance. The small ones were not harmful but there were the large furry ones known as tarantula or bird eating spiders and these could be very dangerous if they bit you. They were one of the most scary members of the insect world and could have a leg span the size of a soup plate and move with great rapidity. They gave no warning of their approach and turned up in the most alarming places. By the path leading to the hospital there was a very large tree which always had one of these spiders resting on its trunk. I used to pass that tree as fast as I could!

Cockroaches were a menace; large, shiny mahogany-brown chaps with long, waving antennae. They took up residence in our kitchen cook houses; up and down the shelves they went, into the pots and pans, and played hide and seek round the dishes. These scenes generally took place at night. A sudden light revealed them all scurrying to take cover. Apart from the kitchen cook house, they spent their day time hours congregating in cupboards, drawers and in every dark nook or cranny they could find. They ate paint off the picture frames and furniture; they ate covers off our books and even fancied a bit of clothing from time to time. Cockroaches certainly played a great part in day to day life!

What about ants; there were a great variety of ants. Little brown ones got into bowls of food if left uncovered, in fact it was necessary to keep food in a little gauze covered 'larder' cupboard on the balcony with the legs standing in tins of paraffin.

Then there were the driver ants that would march in long columns from their forest nest at night to their chosen targets. These could be chicken houses, goat sheds or even the home. Then they would devour all edible 'meat'. In the home, all living insects would be killed and transported in bite size pieces back to their nest. To stay in your house at night during such an invasion would be quite impossible unless you wished to be eaten alive!

Then there were the termites, also known as white ants, who always travelled away from the light. These ants built enormous nests, known as anthills, which could be as tall as 10 feet high. These hills contained a maze of passages and a central chamber for the queen ant. The worker ants were always on the move and specialised in destroying the wood and thatch of our bungalows, making long, narrow underground tunnels from the anthill to their targets. Hence it was necessary to build the bungalows on stone pillars upon which were wide sheets of metal. They would creep along, inside their tunnels, constructing as they went, but never came into the light themselves. If they did get into the bungalows, they would soon devour books, clothing and any wooden structures. On one occasion when Winnie was away, and her little organ was left in the store, we found that the termites had devoured the contents!

At certain times of the year the nuptial flight would take place, when the ants took off in droves to create new colonies. Should one forget to close the gauze covered doors for any reason, they, attracted by the hurricane light, would enter in and make a tasty addition to the soup!

The gauze covered windows and doors on our bungalows were really there to prevent the entry of various other insects, particularly the mosquito, transmitters of the malarial germs which caused the death of so many people. Other intruders were elephant flies, millipedes and mason wasps. These wasps seemed to take a delight in constructing their mud houses under the tables and chairs.

The praying mantis, with front legs lifted as if in prayer and with a head that could turn round at all angles, was a fascinating insect to observe.. But those front legs were also adapted for seizing and holding its prey. Within its natural environment it could however, be very viscous, often killing and eating other insects and even small lizards. The female of the species has been known to kill and eat her own 'husband' becoming fierce and annoyed, bristling up its wings and attacking him with her sharp jaws!

Indeed insect life took some getting used to and seemed to cause far more trouble than the big game of Africa.

There were some beautiful birds to be seen, especially when one was travelling up a creek to a village in the heart of the forest. Brightly coloured kingfishers, beautiful pure white egrets, herons and bright weaver birds that often killed palm trees by stripping off leaves to make their woven nests. The palm tree is a great asset to the Congolese living in the forest. It supplies nuts, oil, roofing in the form of ndele for their houses and palm prongs to make sweeping brooms. Also, deep in the heart of the palm tree is a hard, white vegetable. Wine too, is made from the palm, and this can be a very intoxicating drink. One man was brought in to the hospital drunk from this wine and it took him three days to come round!

The hunters always kept hunting dogs known as basengi hounds but game in the forest was becoming more and more scarce because the animals had been over hunted. However, wild pig, mbokolo (small antelope) and monkeys were a good source of protein in the diet.

There were crocodiles in the lake, but not near the beach at Tondo. We were always warned not to go too far out into the lake when swimming. There were also small crocodiles in the creeks. We often bought crocodile to use in the feeding programmes; they were very tasty and the children loved them.

Sheep and goats were kept in abundance in the villages, but the people were very reluctant to sell them to us as they could get such good prices for them in Mbandaka or Kinshasa.

There are so many more creatures to consider. Lizards with their quaint system of shedding their tails when attacked, but were quite harmless little creatures. Then the rats; these creatures could be very upsetting. They could be very big compared with 'English' rats; some as long as 24 inches from nose to tail tip. We had a white patient convalescing with us at one time. In the night a rat decided to descend from the ceiling and landed right into her glass of water. She soon returned to her home and we never saw her again!"

There were however, other accidents and emergencies in which Mary was involved apart from medical cases.

"We were returning from a village where we had done an ante-natal clinic, also baby and adult clinics. It was late, and following a storm, the road was very muddy and slippery. The Land Rover skidded and the wheels sped round in the mud. I was afraid it was going to topple over so decided to get out and try to wade through the mud. The result was that I slipped and landed flat on my face in the mud! In the meantime the others got safely through in the Land Rover. O ye of little faith!!

One day a hurricane with winds of up to 70-80 mph battered Tondo. It was very frightening at the time. Before the very worst of the storm people had sheltered in their houses, albeit some of them quite flimsy. Many of the patients in the hospital were very frightened. Some stayed and braved the storm, others tried to find shelter in friend's houses. It was a wonder that nobody was killed, as pieces of galvanised tin from the roofs were flying everywhere and trees were falling too. When the storm eventually abated, we went out to find out how much damage was done. Many of the roofing tins of the hospital were taken off and rain was pouring through. We did a roll call to find out where every patient was and if they were safe. Some patients had minor injuries but nothing too serious. The roof covering our linen store was completely taken off and all the linen was completely sodden. In the morning when the sun eventually tried to shine, we had a drying out operation. Sheets, blankets and all our theatre linen was spread out to dry. Of course there are always people taking advantage of this and quite a bit 'disappeared.' Fortunately, the Pharmacy was not affected so all our medicines were high and dry. We sent a gang of workmen out to remove trees which had fallen down over the road into Tondo.

Mr Lyn Collis, our missionary builder, was building a new secondary school at Tondo at the time, so he and his workmen soon started on the essential repairs. The church also suffered the loss of some of the roofing and this they also repaired.

The following week as we walked through the village, we spotted numerous new chicken pens made with bits of our hospital roof! We were only too pleased that it was put to good use. After it was all over, we had a service of thanksgiving to praise our Lord that no lives were lost and to thank and praise Him for His care and protection at that time."

All these experiences and the growing confidence Mary had with the people, built up to a developing trust and faith in all that the missionaries were doing for the people in this area of the Congo. However, unrest was beginning to be noticed, and it was not long before repercussions were to be felt amongst Congolese and European together. Mary was now prepared for the outcome.

———————

Chapter 9

CONGO CRISES

So we say with confidence, "The Lord is my Helper; I will not be afraid.
What can man do to me?"
Hebrews 13v6 (NIV)

Angry tribe arrives at hospital

In 1958 Mary returned to the UK for furlough, then to Antwerp in
Belgium to complete a Tropical Medicine course.. She returned to Congo
a year later and went for a few months to the Baptist Hospital at Bolobo
where they needed some medical help at the time. Then at the end of
the year she moved back to Tondo, together with Arnold and Marjorie
Page and Grace Lowman.

Unrest was developing throughout the Congo during these years and
one began to be aware of more and more disturbances. In fact, just
before the Burtons left in 1956, there had been the first signs of unrest
and an increasing awareness that the once peaceful and prosperous
land of the Belgian Congo was starting to pass through the upheaval of
what would eventually be the birth of a new independent nation.

This particular event had happened one evening. Men with guns and machetes arrived at the hospital proclaiming that they intended killing all patients belonging to a certain tribe. A cyclist was hastily despatched to the nearby State Post of Bikoro to let the Administrator know what was happening. James, in the meantime went down to confront the invaders; a motley crowd of youths, dressed in an assortment of so called 'uniforms', tattered camouflaged jackets, torn shirts and shorts or just a loin cloth decorated with bits of fur. Some carried guns, other machetes. James explained how sick these people in the hospital were and how we were here to help them.. Then, as a truck load of trained soldiers, together with a Belgian officer suddenly arrived from the State Post, the rag-tag 'army' of young rebels melted away into the surrounding forest!

"I thought I had better come over myself," said the officer, "We are beginning to get trouble from these bands of undisciplined youths."

Life in the Congo was starting to change. It would never be quite the same again. What did the future hold for the young Congolese Church; so many missionaries had come to help train and serve?

Mary goes on to describe how things continued to deteriorate.

"Many small political parties were springing up, each with a desire to run the whole country. They were tribal political parties. There were about 200 different tribal languages and different customs between those in the south east of Congo and those in the far north eastern areas. For anyone to successfully govern such a large country with vast differences in customs and languages was indeed a mammoth task. No one had been trained to take over government. They had only been trained to a point where they were useful in government offices, but it would need another 10 years to train them properly for Independence.

Pressure was put on the Belgian Government to hand over, but wisely the Belgians just offered to give them further training with this in view. But even a lower offer of 5 years was rejected and the country was in chaos. The Belgians sent their wives and children home but sadly, many Belgian men were later massacred in the conflict. Communication between Leopoldville had broken down and at that

time, there were just four of us at Tondo; Arnold and Marjorie Page, Grace Lowman and myself.

News of unrest throughout the Congo continued with more and more disturbance. The hospital at Tondo however, was busier than ever, as people relied more and more on the services available there. These people too, were under considerable stress and fear as the atmosphere of unrest affected many of the villages. Stirrings of trouble in other parts of the Congo however, were slow to really affect Tondo in any serious way. But there was a further disturbing incident when a group of 'soldiers approached the hospital again some while after the Burtons had left.

An army truck drove into Tondo with about 20 'soldiers' armed with fixed bayonets. They came to search our houses to see if we had any rifles or bullets. We had been offered rifles from IRSAC (a Belgian Scientific Centre) to protect ourselves, but we had declined the offer. We felt we were much safer without being armed. I was alone at the hospital at the time and one of them came with an officer to harass me while I was doing a ward round. The patients were very frightened. I trusted God to help me and to say the right things.. At this point the soldier turned to the officer and said, "Leave this woman alone. She recently saved the life of my son who was dying of dysentery." So they quietly left! Looking back, I realise it was a miracle that the child had lived; so many of the children die of dysentery. God was certainly with me.

The 'soldiers' also went into the store of the Pages, looking for bullets; they were sure we had some somewhere. At one point a soldier snatched a box from the shelf and shouted, 'Cartouche, cartouche.' (bullets, bullets) On further investigation, the senior officer replied, 'Stupide, ces les articles d'hygiene!'

They eventually left in the truck with their fixed bayonets still at the ready. In the evening the Congolese folks came round to our houses with gifts of food – one of their customs when someone has had a traumatic time. They really are lovable people.

So during the years 1957-1960 one sensed a general atmosphere of growing unrest. There were certain families living in the villages across the lake who were becoming antagonistic to white folks and we sensed that trouble could be a problem in the future. Many African countries were now being given Independence and quite naturally, the Congolese wanted their Independence too. Sadly, only the elite understood what Independence meant. In our area, amongst the remote Congo villages, they had no idea what it was all about. One day I met a lady with a huge basket on her back, walking along the road. She told me she was going to Mbandaka to collect her 'Independence!'

To the majority of older school boys in Tondo, Independence would mean that their fathers would be able to live in big houses, own big American cars and have several wives. The boys would have expensive clothes to wear and wouldn't have to bother about working too hard at school!

The months leading up to Independence was a time of mixed feelings and of great apprehension as to our future service in Congo due to the element of anti-white feelings in the district. We had every reason to be a little fearful.

Then we heard that Lumumba, of the Movement Nationale Congolese, had become President of the country and that Independence Day had finally been fixed for June 30th 1960. It was a great day of rejoicing throughout the Congo; a day of national celebration.

We celebrated the day with our Congolese friends. They organised a feast with us all together on the lawn overlooking the lake. Nurses, school teachers, pastors and village teachers, all came. We feasted on turtle, monkey and crocodile meat and manioc-kwanga (root vegetable pounded into a sticky dough and then rolled into sausage-like shapes, wrapped in banana leaves and steamed over a wood-burning fire) Once cooked, kwanga was grey in colour and tasted like glue! I could not eat it, but later on, when food supplies were short, I acquired quite a taste for it. We also had cooked rice and pondu (a green vegetable from leaves of the kwanga plant, cooked in palm oil). Then there was local fish that had been dried, also cooked in palm oil. For dessert there were fried caterpillars – a Congolese delicacy!

President Mobutu's programme of Authenticity now included total responsibility for Congolese to be in charge of all Institutes including

Mission hospitals and schools. The country was renamed The Republic of Zaire. All names of towns were changed to African names. Leopoldville the capital became Kinshasa, Coquilhatville became Mbandaka and Stanleyville became Kisangani. All public services were very much run down and we couldn't rely on mail any more. There were very few stores available in the city shops and on one occasion all we could get were tins of pilchards. We ate them in every conceivable way and soon felt that we began to look like pilchards! Although living by the lake, very little fish was available, because the strict control the Belgians had had of not taking small fish out of the lake, was now being ignored by the people, so the fish stock was now depleted as a result. If they did make a good catch it was dried and taken to Mbandaka market where the people could make a lot more money from it.

Everything had to be essentially African and all Congolese were required to adopt African names. We could not call any of our Congolese friends by their Christian names any more. The Zairarian girls were no longer able to wear slacks or jeans; they had to resort to African dress. Incidentally, European women were not able to wear trousers either!

Tondo Hospital had to be changed from Hopital Tremont, named originally after an American town that had actually paid for the hospital building. The name was changed to Lopital Tondo.

The currency was changed from francs and cents to zaires and makutu. This was a great hardship for many living in the forest, who, not having access to banks in the cities, buried all their savings under the floor of their houses.

Mongu (his Christian name Raymond, no longer allowed) now became Director of Tondo Secondary School, in place of Miss Winifred Hadden, who was transferred up river to Yalemba. I was no longer Directrice of Lopital Tondo. Ikoma (Denis) became Director of the hospital. He was an excellent nurse and had initially been trained by Dr Burton in surgery procedures too. At that time, we could not have envisaged a time when we would no longer be needed in the operating theatre. Now I only went when Ikoma asked for my help.

As a result of all the upheaval and drastic changes, many people lost a great deal of money and could not afford to pay for hospital treatment. So we set up a system of barter. Eggs, chickens, ducks, peanuts and fruit, accepted for out patients, medicines, consultations and minor surgery. Monkey, crocodile, turtle, antelope and large fish for major surgery. Then all foods were used to feed children and the elderly on our Feeding Programmes. People earning salaries however, were requested to pay cash. We needed this to pay salaries and hospital bills.

By 1961 there was an uneasy relationship between us and the Congolese nursing staff. Until this time we had both worked on a rota of being on call at night for any emergency that came in. However, now they decided that they would no longer be on call at night and that we should be on call every night. Of course this was not possible, but we were quite willing to take our full share. Two of the nurses complained to the State officials (now Zaireans) about us. We had always worked in complete harmony up until now and Ikoma did not support the nurses' complaints. However, we were called to go to the State office at Bikoro, about 20 kilometres away. Here the matter was to be judged. It was necessary for us to obey the 'command.'

Judgement was made in favour of the nurses and we were prevented from returning to Tondo. (Grace Lowman was with me) Instead, we were locked up as prisoners in a small hut. Outside was a soldier on guard with a fixed bayonet. It was not a very easy situation to accept but we had no option. We prayed and asked the Lord to undertake for us. After a few hours our guard obviously needed to consider his own personal needs according to nature! There being no replacement, he looked around, then quickly disappeared into the surrounding forest.

"Quick," said Grace who was with me, together with our driver, "The Land Rover is still there. Lets make a dash for it!"

So, heaving our united strength against the flimsy door, we escaped. We all jumped rapidly into the Land Rover and praised the Lord that the key was still in the ignition! We then made off at full speed towards Mbandaka where we knew that we could get legal advice. The road was particularly bad that day as there had been a tropical storm the night before. The Land Rover slipped and slithered and several times almost landed in the ditch. However, we did make it and were welcomed by the

American Disciples of Christ missionaries. The Congolese Head of the Mission was there; a fine Christian man. He himself went to see the Governor, and we were immediately exonerated of doing anything wrong. They sent a very stern letter back to our nurses, reminding them that our help was sorely needed in the country at this time.

When we finally met up with the nurses on our return, they came out to greet us with open arms. The Congolese never held a grudge."

So the Congo, now the Republic of Zaire, started into a new phase and the missionaries had to fit into a different pattern. This would take time and as Mary readjusted her role in the hospital programme, she was still fully occupied until she left for Furlough in 1963.

Chapter 10

THE CRISIS DEEPENS

He who dwells in the shelter of the Most High will rest in the shadow
of the Almighty.
I will say of the Lord, "He is my refuge and my fortress, my God, in
whom I trust."
Psalm 91v1-2. (NIV)

As the Congo endeavoured to settle down following the Independence
uprising of 1960, there continued to be an atmosphere of unrest and
tribal disturbances. More and more anxious news emerged from every
corner of the Congo. Reports of houses and villages burning, of long
nights of terror and days filled with forebodings. Who was responsible
for all these acts?

From jungle hideouts wild bands of young men, it seemed, were
causing most of the violence that was now erupting; idle young men,
disillusioned that Independence made them neither wise nor wealthy
as they had been promised. So they had banned into units of a loose-
knit organisation called 'Jeunesse'. Undisciplined and not knowing
their own purpose, they robbed, pillaged, threatened, tortured, killed
and destroyed. They struck out to terrorise villages, Government Posts
and Mission stations. Africans and foreigners alike, were their victims. It
eventually became apparent however, that these were more than
disenchanted youths; they were the makings of a growing army which
in due course began to formulate and become known as the 'Simba'
army, comprised of primitive tribesmen.

The country was in turmoil; people far and wide, both Congolese,
European or anyone else not directly involved in the Rebellion, began to
feel the strain and tension that was penetrating everywhere. News was
slow to filter through to the outside world, because of a breakdown in
communications. But as the situation became worse, there were reports
of raids on Belgian State Posts and Plantations, as well as raids on both
Catholic and Protestant Mission stations.

This was the situation in 1964 when Mary returned from furlough, and she, together with the other missionaries now at Tondo, had to get to terms with a very disturbed and different future. Mary continues her story of the coming months after her return.

"After Independence in 1960 the country really never settled down. At the beginning of 1965 we were starting to feel the effects of the Simba uprising. It was the population in the north eastern part of the country who were so cruelly treated by the Simba's. The word Simba means Lion. Many young people were involved, and many of their atrocities were performed whilst under the influence of drugs. Sadly, many missionaries, both Catholic and Protestant, were to die cruelly at their hands, including children too. The rebels were gradually spreading towards the south eastern parts of the country. There was a great deal of unrest. All expatriates were under suspicion and many were taken prisoner.

At Tondo, we were not directly affected. However, the Simbas did send a group of their men to Nzalakenga, some 20 kilometres from Tondo, to try to win the folks over to their cause. They were overrun by the people and sent away; the house they had been living in was burnt down. This incident was a bit too near for comfort! At the time I was repainting the inside of the house and I wondered if I was doing it for myself or for the rebels!

We were told to listen to the World Overseas programme of the BBC, and one day we were advised to 'take a holiday'! We learnt that our BMS wives and children had already been sent home; we had not received the advice at Tondo, owing to a breakdown in communications from Kinshasa.

"Here we sit like birds in the wilderness," exclaimed Grace!

The Congolese were our friends and colleagues and assured us of their protection what ever happened. Infact, one day a group of Batwa folks came and told us of a plan they had compiled to take us deep into the forest and hide us if necessary. We trusted them and told them that if a need arose we would be very grateful for their help. But we remained at Tondo, trusting in God to keep us and our Congolese folk safe. One day, in our morning meditations we were given a verse from Isaiah chapter 52v12. 'For ye shall not go out with haste, nor go by flight; for the Lord will go before you.' So in faith we carried on.

The staff at Tondo at that time, comprised Grace Lowman and myself, together with Dr Lewis Mullins, now due to leave; his wife and children had already left. This would mean that Grace and myself would be the only ones left.

By now the rebels had reached Boende; Mbandaka our nearest town was their next target. If they took this town we would have no means of getting out, as we depended on the river boats and the Airport. There would be no other means of escape.

The BMS were unable to find another doctor or male missionary to come to Tondo, and were not prepared to leave two single ladies on their own during these unsettled days. So the decision was made to withdraw all missionaries from Tondo for the time being at any rate. Our Congolese friends were devastated, but we, and they, both knew that if we stayed, they too would have been put in grave danger trying to protect us. It was a great sorrow to me, after 10 years at Tondo, to have to leave.

The hospital buildings, equipment and medicines, had to be handed over to the church and they would just run it as a dispensary and be responsible for the administration. I was informed from our Field Secretary, Mr Drake, that for the moment, there was no work for me with the BMS, owing to the evacuation of Bolobo, Yakusu and Yalemba. It was suggested that I approach one of the other missions for the time being.

So, Grace Lowman and I left Tondo on Friday March 5th 1965, heading for Mbandaka, where we stayed with the American Disciples of Christ in Congo Mission. Here we waited for instructions.

Grace was offered a job to do church work at Lulongo with the Congo Balobo Mission; an English Mission. They had no work for me as both of their hospitals were now in rebel hands. However, the Disciples of Christ Mission offered me a job at Lotumbe, situated on the River Momboyo, a tributary of the River Congo, where they had a doctor but no nurse. Dr Ross had built a new hospital with a complete maternity unit but with no nurse to work in it, as at that time not many American nurses were trained as midwives. BMS were quite happy about this arrangement because the hospital there had a small mission plane, and Dr Ross had his own little Cessna plane, so if necessary, evacuation would be possible, also they were in contact with Kinshasa and the outside world by radio. Lulongo, where Grace was posted, was not too far away, so both Grace and I could be evacuated together if necessary. Both French and Lingala were spoken at Lotumbe and Lulongo, so we did not have to learn a new language."

Another chapter in Mary's life was about to begin. It was quite a cultural shock leaving Tondo and then working at an American mission, but she was soon to realise how valuable her work there was to be.

———————

Chapter 11

SHELTERED FROM THE STORM

God is our refuge and strength, a very present help in trouble.
Psalm 46v1 (AV)

Thus as turmoil continued to disrupt the Congo, the remaining missionaries were distributed around the various mission centres, applicable to their particular gifting. Mary was so fortunate to be able to go to the American Disciples of Christ Mission at Lotumbe, where her medical knowledge was going to be such an asset to the folk there. She continues to tell us about her experiences over the next two years.

Cessna Mission Plane takes off

"So, on March 29th 1965 I flew with Dr John Ross to Lotumbe. I've never been in such a small plane before; it was fascinating looking down into the deep forest and seeing elephants grazing with their young. In days to come I would be going with Dr John in the Cessna plane to do medical work with him on several occasions in the outlying districts. Often, when we wanted to bring a seriously ill patient back to the hospital with us, they and the family would refuse, because they were frightened to come by plane. It would have then taken them two or more days to come by canoe.

When we arrived at Lotumbe, I was given a very warm welcome by Mrs Mabel Ross, Congolese friends and missionary colleagues. The next day, Dr John took me to see the hospital. He showed me the Maternity Department and said,

"Mary, here are the keys; it is fully equipped, and all yours to do what you like with it."

There had been no midwifery available for the folks at Lotumbe before. I took on four girls from the Secondary School and planned a full two year midwifery course for them. At the end of two years all four of them received their certificates, and they were recognised by the State as fully qualified midwives.

Girl's Graduation Day - Lotumbe

In due course an American nurse arrived and we lived and worked together. Dorothy being responsible for the operating theatre and general wards, while I concentrated on the Midwifery block. We had great fun living together and learning each others languages!. We put a Union Jack on the Maternity block and stars and stripes on the General ward!

Dr John had to be away from the station at frequent intervals, as he was responsible for all the medical work of the mission on other stations too. Then Dorothy and I were left to run the hospital on our own.

One day a man arrived who had been in a fight. Dr John had already left for a business trip to Mbandaka. Dorothy and I were both feeling a bit tired so decided to have an early night. At that point the nurse from the hospital came rushing down the path to our house.

"Come quickly," he said, "A fight has taken place in the village and they have brought a wounded man in."

So we rushed to the hospital and found the entrance to the main wards and the theatre so crowded with people wailing and screaming, that we literally had to push our way in. There in the theatre was Imbolo, our head theatre nurse, with the patient on the table. A horrible sight met our eyes, with blood spurting everywhere. He had been in a fight with knives, with another man. He had seventeen wounds; one in the neck, which miraculously just missed the jugular vein. There was another one across his back about fourteen inches long and one inch deep, which went right through muscle, almost to the bone. A third under his armpit, two more across his chest, one on the eyebrow and cheek, fortunately missing the eye. There were further deep cuts on both hands between the thumb and forefinger and many other smaller wounds which also needed to be sutured.

We didn't have time to stop and pray before starting work as we usually did, but silently prayed as we worked. Imbolo and I repaired the serious wounds and Dorothy the smaller ones. It was now 8pm but it was midnight before we finally put the last suture in and miraculously our patient was still alive. He was put in a side ward with an intravenous drip and a night nurse to monitor him – No intensive care ward in this hospital!

Dorothy and I had just reached our house when a night nurse rushed down again.

"Bamama, come quickly. They have just brought the second man in who was in the fight."

So back to work we went. This man had an eight inch wound across his waist, and his left thumb was nearly severed off. We put him in a ward at the other end of the hospital, well away from the first man. We tried to separate the relatives from both families as much as possible, to prevent another fight! We eventually crawled into bed at 3am; so much for our early night!!

Next morning the police came to sort out the palaver; one woman and two men were put into prison. All knives and spears possessed by patients and relatives were confiscated.

On another occasion while Dr John was away, we had a man with acute abdominal pain; query appendicitis. Fortunately a Pastor from Flandria was going home. There was a State doctor at Flandria. The Pastor agreed to take the patient and his relatives in his boat which had an outboard motor. We arranged for one of our nurses to go with them. Everyone was at the beach all ready to leave when the nurse came running up to us and said that they could not find the patient! We understood that the relatives were bringing him down on a stretcher. However, on investigation, we discovered that the patient had decided that he would rather die than pay the Pastor for the cost of the outboard! Then, after much persuasion that life was better than death, he agreed to go.

When Dorothy and I were having lunch on the veranda, we saw someone hobbling down the path to the beach. The relatives were now so fed up with him that they refused to carry him on the stretcher! He did eventually arrive at Flandria where he was operated on successfully, and from relatives reports we presume it was a case of appendicitis. They told us that the doctor had removed a little 'worm' from his tummy!

There was a message from Dr John one morning.

"Mary, come at once to the theatre."

I dropped everything and rushed over. He was operating on a Batwa man suffering from elephantiasis – enormous enlargement of the scrotum – infact in this case the scrotum nearly reached the ground! It was a long operation with all hands on deck and blood everywhere as vessels were tied off. A relative was found who was willing to give blood for a transfusion. The operation took 3 hours but the man recovered.

Soon after all this we heard angry voices outside, including the one who had given the blood.

"We demand the blood of our relative back," they cried.

A riot was imminent, but the head nurse quickly quelled the angry mob, threatened them and quietened them down. The man made a good recovery but the day before he was due to be discharged, he disappeared in the night together with all his relatives. This was one way of getting out of paying the bill!!

One morning, just as Dr John and Mrs Ross and Dorothy were about to take off in the small mission Cessna plane to go to Mbandaka for a shopping trip – no convenient store round the corner – a patient was brought into maternity. A live baby had been delivered in the village but the mother was bleeding profusely. I realised that only part of the placenta had come away, due to meddlesome midwifery in the village. So I sent a quick SOS to Dr John to come before he left. They were anxious to get away, so he sent a message back.

"Don't worry, Mary, I know you will cope!"

With God's help I did, by doing a manual removal of the rest of the afterbirth. Mother and baby made a good recovery, thanks to answered prayer. So often when alone on a mission station we came face to face with a difficult case and then looked up all the text books we had. When we got to the point our patient had reached, the text book merely said, 'Send for the doctor!' When said doctor is hundreds of miles away, our only hope was the wonder working power of prayer.

I was still officially a missionary with BMS and once a year had to attend the regional Church Conference. One such occasion stands out in my memory. Dr John flew me to Mbandaka where I met up with Grace Lowman again. We then caught the river boat that was going to Bolobo where the Conference was to be held. There were seven of us on the boat, including Congolese Pastors. Supper on board consisted of meat that was so tough that even our knives would not cut it. 'This must be elephant meat,' we thought. The Pastors however, tore it apart with their hands and ate it, but Grace and I declined!

We all had first class tickets, so were entitled to cabin accommodation. But for seven of us there was only one cabin available. The Pastors very graciously insisted that Grace and I should have it. They slept in the bar on armchairs. Fortunately the bar had run out of beer, so there were no other passengers.

The next day was Sunday and we were happy to receive permission from the Captain to hold a church service in the Bar; it was crammed full of passengers. Pastor Mompoko from Tondo led the service and Grace gave the address.

We eventually arrived at Lukolela where we were picking up several more delegates, both English and Congolese. We arrived at Bolobo at 7pm when it was dark, but fortunately a moonlit night. Then our troubles started! Only the noses of the barges attached to the boat pulled into the beach. The back of the boat where we were, was about 100 yards from the shore. Also, as our boat approached, many canoes came out from Bolobo to meet us. They were selling their wares of fish, bananas, plantains, kwanga, manioc etc. This meant that the boat couldn't get anywhere near the beach. A narrow plank as a gangway was put down at the far end of the barges. For us to get to it would be impossible.

"How are we expected to clamber over that lot?" asked Grace, as we viewed the scene. 'That lot' involved milling crowds, stacks and stacks of dried fish and kwanga, together with a motley group of undisciplined goats and sheep. With all our luggage we just couldn't make it.

As we stood looking out over some 100 yards of water, wondering how we were going to cross it, a boat official suddenly appeared. He told us to get off the boat immediately as they were just about to leave!! We identified with this command, but how were we expected to find our way?

After much shouting, imploring and yelling, we managed to get a woman with a canoe to come alongside the barge. She agreed to take us to the beach. To get into her flimsy canoe involved a six foot drop down the side of the barge. When all of my 10 stone dropped down into it, the canoe very nearly sank! Pastor Mompoko, who had been first off the boat, managed to get another canoe and worked very hard ferrying other passengers and all our luggage off the boat. Grace and I were in a very wobbly canoe and the woman who was paddling us was more interested in selling her goods, so she kept stopping to yell to her friends. Each time she stopped the canoe rocked perilously and we were nearly tipped into the water. Grace was hugging a radio and I was holding a typewriter above my head so that it wouldn't get wet if we descended into the river.

Eventually the woman got us almost to the shore but because of the water hyacinth weed she couldn't get any nearer, so we had to wade to the shore with the water nearly up to our knees.

By the time we were all assembled on the shore, it was quite dark, and then we discovered we were not on the main Bolobo beach anyhow! It was very muddy and we couldn't find a way out. Then one of the Pastors told us all to shout loudly together for help, to the Congolese folks at Bolobo and, yes, they heard us and they did come to rescue us!

Then, just as we were about to leave, we remembered that we had left a case of tinned corn beef on the boat. This was for feeding the Conference! Pastor Mompoko quickly grabbed a canoe and raced back to the boat. He just managed to get someone to drop it off into the canoe, before they finally left. Apparently the Bolobo folks were not expecting us to arrive until the following day in our own outboard motor boat.

All the Bolobo missionary staff had been evacuated, but the Conference was held there to encourage the Christians. The missionaries had left keys to their houses and food stores. Grace and I were located a house but the African in charge of it wouldn't let us in until the next day; he said he hadn't cleaned it! So we spent the night crammed into another house with two other delegates, where there were only two beds. By then it was 9.30pm and we were so tired we didn't care whether we slept on the floor or even on a clothes line!

During the night we heard what we thought was gunfire and we were quite scared. In the morning we discovered that there was a mango tree right by the house and the fruit bats had spent the night dropping mangos on the tin roof! For breakfast we had dried apple rings as that was all that was left in the food store.

We had a very good Conference and indications were made that I would possibly be able to return to Tondo after my next furlough. The Disciples of Christ Mission wanted me to transfer to their Mission and work for them permanently (it would be a much higher salary) But my heart was with the people at Tondo and BMS. No way did I even want to think about leaving them.

However, I did appreciate and enjoy my two years at Lotumbe and made many friends amongst the Congolese folks there. I thanked our Lord for the new experiences and friends, and for protecting us all during those very disturbing years. However, my heart was always at Tondo; I just longed to be back."

So Mary's time at Lotumbe came to an end. She had gained a wealth of experience during her stay and this would put her in good stead for the outstanding responsibilities that were to face her soon after returning to Tondo. Now was the time for another furlough and a well deserved rest, after a very traumatic term of service for her Lord and Master.

Chapter 12

MAMA MALIA RETURNS FROM FURLOUGH

And great multitudes came unto Him, having with them those that
were lame, blind, dumb, maimed, and many others, and cast them
down at Jesus' feet; and He healed them.
Matthew 15v30 (AV)

Although the atmosphere in Congo began to quieten, there was still a great amount of restlessness and disruption throughout the country. The Congo would never be the same again. Stories about individual cases in the north east of Congo began to emerge. Missionaries dragged from their beds in the middle of the night and pulled into the forest; some tortured, humiliated or even massacred. Hospitals raided and equipment stolen. A doctor actually operating on a 'Simba' soldier, was dragged out of the theatre, massacred and thrown into the river; his wife and children too, similarly treated. Thirty nine missionaries colleagues, martyred for Jesus. Catholic nuns and priests were not exempt.

The city of Kisangani fell into the hands of the rebel army and 1600 European, American and Asian foreigners were held hostage. Then, as the United Nation paratroops finally dropped from the sky to rescue them, the Simbas launched out in a final blood-thirsty stampede, aiming their weapons into a crowd of 250 human targets. Stunned, humiliated prisoners, screams of terror and shrieks of sudden pain filled the streets. People ran, others stood in bewilderment. Lives were lost minutes before the paratroops could arrive to rescue them. This was the appalling situation that covered those years following Independence.

As the main trouble was in the north east of Congo, Tondo was not directly involved in these terrible atrocities. However, Mary continued the work she had been commissioned to do, obeying a God who wanted her to share the love of Jesus with those who had never heard. As she returned to Congo in 1968, her first consignment was to spend six months in Kinshasa the capital, working in a busy dispensary. She explains about her time here, before returning to Tondo later in the year.

"My journey back to Congo seems such a long while ago and now I am settling down to life in the 'Big City' and it is vastly different from anything I have been used to before.. I have never been in such a busy and demanding job as this one. The need is great; the people in the area where we hold our dispensary are very poor, and really sick. There is a wonderful opportunity of preaching the Gospel to them as we minister to their bodily needs. The dispensary is held in a bungalow which used to house one of our Pastors, but his family grew in numbers so they had to build him a new house.

After working in a somewhat spacious hospital, I find that we are very cramped here, and seem to be on top of each other all the time. We average about 2500 consultations a month plus very busy baby and antenatal clinics each week. In my team of workers I have 4 Congolese nurses, a clerk and one workman, who acts as a policeman and keeps the queues of folks in order.

My one problem is transport, as without a car life is difficult. The dispensary is half an hours walk away; good for me, but I can't afford that two hours each day. Now the church have bought me a bicycle so I cycle to and fro. There are cycle paths most of the way and for about 500 yards one has to pass the open market and wend ones way through the crowds and vendors. I'm getting on quite friendly terms with the store holders and they usually cut the price for me when I buy from them. But the work at St Jeans Dispensary is not without its troubles. It is a terrific temptation for the nurses to be handling drugs each day, as even for one tablet they could obtain quite a sum of money. The cost of living in Kinshasa is very high and salary rates are not rising in proportion.

During my time in Kinshasa there was a great deal of trouble at Tondo from a break away group led by Nzee Samuel. This has begun to settle but is by no means stable. They tell me that all the houses are in need of repair."

So after two years Mary was ready to return to Tondo. She received a wonderfully warm welcome from the people there. Under Congolese supervision the work of the Mission had continued, but now Mary had to adjust to a new pattern in the hospital schedule. The daily routine was as busy as ever with desperate people seeking all the help and comfort that the hospital was able to give. Apart from the regular routine and emergency medical cases, there were many disabled people too. These all had to be fitted into the programme. For a while, Mary was on her own at Tondo, which meant that she had to carry out medical procedures that would normally be done by the doctor. She removed toe nails, bisected abscesses, dealt with complicated gynaecological cases and of course, sutured wounds. Listen to Mary's reports on some of these cases.

"It had been raining all day and at 11pm I had a call to go to the hospital. I guessed that something serious had happened as there was much wailing, with crowds of folks making their way to the hospital. The patient was somewhere, being carried in, but there was such a surge of folk and hysteria, I had a job to make my way anywhere near the patient.

I discovered that it was Tata Ikali, a very faithful church member; he was also one of the Education Inspectors in the Province. It appeared that he had gone to Mbandaka to get the money to pay the school teachers their salaries. It was a very dark, wet night. He had acquired a lift in an ancient lorry with poor lights, poor brakes and a driver who had had more to drink than was safe, before driving. Suddenly there was a smash! They went at high speed into a large tree that had fallen across the road. Ikali was thrown through the windscreen and his face was torn to pieces with fragments of glass.

We eventually managed to get him into the theatre where I could begin to repair the damage. We couldn't use a general anaesthetic as we only had oil lamps; no electricity. I sent one of the nurses to Grace Lowman's house, asking her to come with a strong torch for extra light, also to stay and help control the crowds who were all trying to enter the operating theatre. After 5 hours Ikoma and I finished stitching up his face, having put in about 50 sutures, some around the eyes with very fine thread. Against all odds he made a good recovery. The doctor from Bikoro State Post came to see him, and said we had done a good job!

Elima had a very deformed leg and his family sought for advice. Bypassing all the witch doctors in the area, they came by canoe over the lake to Tondo to ask us for help. We could do nothing for his physical condition at Tondo, so we sent him to the Lower Congo district, where there was a large hospital run jointly with British, Swedish and American Protestant Missions. It was known as IME – Institute Medical Evangelique. There he was seen by an orthopaedic surgeon who performed an amputation of the deformed leg and eventually fitted him out with an artificial leg. He was then taught to walk with it without the aid of pole or sticks. Elima and his family were thrilled. When Elima came back to show us his new leg, he was so delighted with it that he wanted to show it off to everyone; he even wore shorts and refused to wear long trousers!

Also when he arrived he proudly showed us a new pair of shoes and white socks. He had never owned a pair of these before; only odd ones given to him by those who were discarding them! One problem for Elima was that he had been advised not to return to live permanently in his own village as it was very damp and swampy and this atmosphere would ruin his artificial leg. So as he was a bright lad we took him on in the hospital as a clerk. He was trained to keep the records and later on he became treasurer, taking all the payments as the patients came in. He was absolutely trustworthy and we never missed one likuta (penny) from the money which he handled.

He worked for us for 20 years and during this time he married a lovely Christian lady and raised a large family. He is now living in retirement at Tondo. Actually, I have just received a letter in the post from him. He now has many grandchildren, 'nkoko' as they call them. He no longer wears shorts!

Many folk are disabled as a result of poliomyelitis contracted in childhood. One lad, Koko, could no longer walk and just crawled along the ground. Also, Mpia, an elderly man disabled and house-bound. Many others also came to us for help.

Our prayers were answered through ECHO (Equipment for Charity Hospitals Overseas) founded by Dr Burton after he left Congo and returned to the UK. ECHO supplied refurbished medical equipment, also drugs at low cost, for missionary hospitals and dispensaries overseas. Dr Burton was also able to supply us with invalid wheel chairs. As a result these people were now released from bondage and were able to visit friends, shop and church, and lead a normal social life. Many of them too, experienced the new life we have in Jesus Christ our Lord.

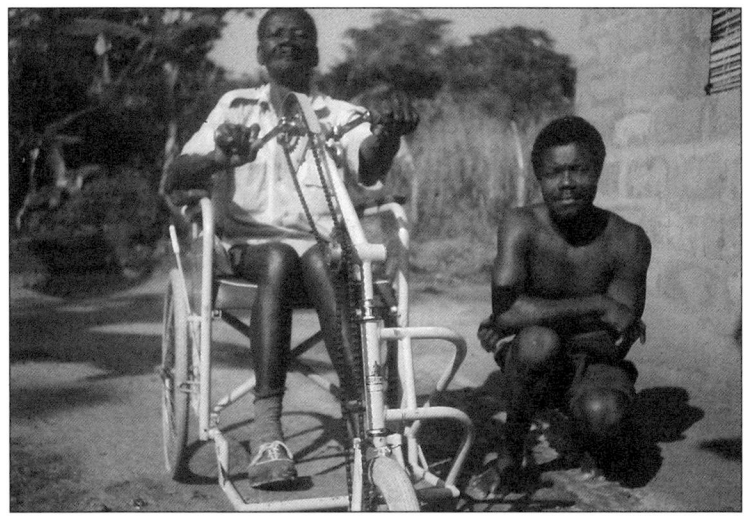
Wheelchair from ECHO

There were many blind folk living around Lake Tumba area and every day, walking through the villages, one saw blind men and women being led by a young lad or girl, the blind person holding one end of the stick and the child in front holding the other end, leading the blind person along. Blindness may be caused by untreated cases of leprosy, river blindness by black fly, glaucoma, untreated cataracts, diabetes mellitus or venereal disease. Some cases however, were congenital.

As a result of a visit from Dr Adrian Hopkins, an Eye Specialist, many patients were treated for glaucoma and cataracts and were given special spectacles to wear. One day some time later, one man came to me and said, 'Mama, these spectacles are no longer any good. I cannot see with them. Can I have a new pair?' I took his old glasses, gave them a good wash and returned them to him. He was delighted and offered to pay for his 'new specs'! I told him that if he regularly washed them, there was no need for new specs. A good sermon illustration which I used later in the church!

Behind the hospital was a Leprosarium where patients suffering from leprosy were segregated. We had quite a little village there. The man in charge of the welfare of the patients was Pastor Nsomo. He did not suffer from the disease himself, but faithfully worked amongst those who did, helping both spiritually and also attending to their every day needs. Those who were able, were given work to do around the mission grounds. In those days 'Dapsone' was the drug of choice, which for the first time in history controlled the disease. Nowadays treatment for leprosy has been dramatically changed. If diagnosed within the first six months of the disease, they can be cured with the 'Multiple Drug Treatment' which involves taking three different drugs a day. In advanced cases the disease can be controlled, but the disabilities remain. They are no longer segregated from the other villagers.

Mama Nsomboli

One remarkable patient in the Leprosarium was Nsomboli. She was a very special patient. She contracted leprosy many years ago and was eventually brought to Tondo by her relatives in a canoe across the lake. They then left her abandoned, lying on the beach at the waters edge. She was found and immediately taken to the Leprosarium, where she was given a little hut made of sun dried mud bricks. She was given new clothes to replace the rags she was wearing, and given daily food for her bodily needs. But most important of all, she was taught about Jesus and His love and care for her. She became a radiant Christian and a great witness in the camp, always ready to help other patients who needed counselling and guidance. As a young missionary, whenever I felt despondent, I would go to old Nsomboli's hut and have a chat with her; I always came away encouraged.

When years later Nsomboli passed into the presence of her Lord and Saviour, we all gathered round her bed in the hospital and instead of the usual wailing and distress, the folk quietly sang hymns. It was such a good witness to the other patients in the ward. How we all missed Nsomboli, grossly disfigured in her face and with no toes and fingers, she had a beautiful spirit which beamed from her dear old face. At her funeral, the people turned out in great numbers to honour her; the church was packed. But not one member of her family were present.

Monzoi was another of our old leprosy patients. He could remember the hospital being built in1924. As far as we know, he had no relatives who visited him; we were his only family.

Mola had a very disfigured face as a result of his leprosy, and he was blind. However, Mola had a lovely singing voice. I remember one Christmas Eve on a moonlight night. We heard a beautiful rendering of 'Silent Night, Holy Night,' being sung. Many of us followed the sound of the singing and came to Mola's house where he was praising his Lord in song and so giving a wonderful testimony."

Many of the cases described in this chapter happened when Mary was actually on her own. What incredible experiences she had and this was only the daily routine. Although the problems of the rebellion did not directly disturb the Tondo district, there were disturbances from time to time, but throughout, the people guarded and protected Mary whenever trouble threatened. Despite her busy schedule, there were yet many other areas in which she was involved.

Chapter 13

CHILDREN IN NEED

Suffer the little children to come unto Me, and forbid them not:
for of such is the Kingdom of God.
Mark 10v14 (AV)

One of the areas that concerned Mary was the subject of Public Health, both in the Mission and in the surrounding district villages. She was particularly aware of the children, the women and the elderly and, over the years, was responsible for many improvements. She developed Feeding Programmes and regular village visits. Let us follow her progress as we hear about her interesting responsibilities.

"My colleague, Wilma Aitchinson, and I prayed about our future role at Tondo.

"Wilma," I said one day, "I feel that we should try to get involved in church work, especially with the women and children which, since Independence, are not given priority."

Wilma agreed and also added, "What about Public Health work in Tondo and the district?"

We both felt the Lord calling us into these possibilities. So after prayerful consideration with Ikoma and Pastor Ngando, who was now head of the station, Wilma and I commenced a routine which continued right until the time I retired in1984. We were both very excited as we planned monthly trips to the villages across the lake to do public health and medical work in the mornings and church work in the afternoon and evenings. One of us to be away from Tondo and visiting villages nearby , by canoe and bicycle. We would take turn about month after month.

Our first priority was to train three lads and three girls who had finished Secondary School, but whose parents couldn't afford to send them on for further training away from home. Public health was completely new to them, and we knew that it would be even harder to convince the folk in the outlying villages of the importance of this. They would listen to their own folk, but new ideas from a 'mondele' (white person) would not always be acceptable. Fortunately, both Wilma and I had all our notes and visual aids with us, which we acquired in Antwerp when we did our Tropical Medicine course before coming to Congo.

We also trained some older women who could come with us to help with the work amongst the women and children. Ecole de Dimanche (Sunday School), women's work and discipleship classes for men and women; all were needed. Arnold and Marjorie Page, together with Grace Lowman, had all visited many of these villages in the past and had laid a wonderful foundation upon which we could build with this post Independence generation.

Our next priority was to visit Boika who was the local dugout canoe maker. We had to have a canoe of our own as we couldn't keep the church and hospital canoes away from Tondo for any length of time. So we went to his little mud hut at the end of the village. We greeted him in the usual way.

"Boika, mbote mingi."

"Mbote, Mama, nsango mini?" (Greetings, what news?) he replied.

"We need a canoe, can you make us one?" we asked.

"Ee Ee, monene boni?" (Yes yes, but how big?)

"Oh big enough to take 15 people plus luggage." We replied.

"Come with me," he said, "And we will chose a tree to fell. There are two trees suitable for making canoes," he continued, "One will make a good canoe which will last a very long time, but if you overturn in the lake, it will sink and you will have nothing to hold on to. There is another tree which will make a good canoe, but it will not last as long as the other, but if you are tipped out of the boat in the middle of the lake, it will float upside down to the surface, and you will have something to hold on to."

We chose the latter, then bargained the price. He asked for 200 Zaires, but we finally settled for 100 Zaires.

"I'll make you six paddles too," he added, "Plus two bailers." So eventually we got our canoe and were ready to set off.

Right from the beginning, the one thing that confronted us was the struggle and pull affecting the people between the witch doctor and the white man's medicine. The witch doctor had a strong influence on the people. They believed in and worshiped the spirits of the departed and if they made them angry, the people would die. If they came to us, they were told, the spirits would be very angry. The native medicines offered by the witch doctor were often the cause of death rather than the original ailment from which the patient was suffering. But occasionally, they did have medicine to cure diseases which we couldn't!

I remember the occasion of a child with terrible conjunctivitis, a severe inflammation of the eye. We tried antibiotics with no result. Then one of the helpers in the hospital called the patient to her house and treated the child's eyes with her own native medicine; there was a cure overnight! In spite of my pleading, she would not tell me what she had used. 'That's my secret,' she said. These cures were a tight secret and would only be handed down from father to son or daughter.

As the Public Health scheme developed, we began to train some of the young village lads to be leaders. A family man with no regular job was preferable, but one who had enough prestige in the village to be looked up to. They came to Tondo in the beginning for a course of lectures in Public Health, then went back to the villages to teach the folk there, by being a shining example in hygiene in their own homes.

We gave them a few aspirin and nivaquine (if available) and they were taught to treat very high fevers. But if the temperature did not come down by the morning, the patient must be sent into the hospital for our advice. The nurse in charge visited the villages regularly, to see if these helpers were doing their job properly. As well as the health workers, we also trained the village girls to be midwives. Eventually, we had health workers in 50 villages.

By this time the State had become aware of the importance of Public Health and set up their own programme. We benefited from this as they sent us quite a lot of equipment and medicines. They also gave us a new paraffin oil run refrigerator, and a microscope for each village."

Mary also had concern for Public Health amongst women and children coming into the hospital.

"We had a trained Congolese midwife at Tondo and we delivered about 250 babies each year in the hospital. But there were many mothers who had their babies in the villages; sometimes at the cost of the baby's or the mother's life. In our Public Health programme we were constantly teaching the need for the women to come to hospital for their confinements, but always the excuse was that they could not afford it.

Tetanus in newborn babies was also a killer. To combat this we gave every mother who attended the ante-natal clinic, a little pack containing a new razor blade with which to cut the cord, sterile tape to tie the cord before cutting, cord dressings and cotton wool. The packs were prepared at the hospital in our sterilizer which resembled a pressure cooker, heated over a camp fire in the hospital kitchen! This procedure reduced the number of babies dying from tetanus, as the cord was normally just cut with a dirty old kitchen knife. The father was delighted to keep the razor blade afterwards!

Included too, in our Public Health programme was the Under Fives Clinic for the children. Here again we found this very discouraging as the mothers were very keen to have their new babies weighed and admired every week, but they were not interested in bringing their older children. Most of the children were very anaemic due to worm infection and attacks of malaria. One child passed 50 worms after being treated. The mothers were very conservative in their eating habits; they wouldn't give the children eggs to eat because they said it would prevent them walking when they grew up! Milk too, was refused because it came from a cow and this was an abomination to them. Meat and fish were very scarce, hence the malnutrition. The children lived on kwanga (manioc) a root vegetable with very little nutrition in it, and pondu, a green vegetable cooked in palm oil.

We tried to teach them that it was the child who had been weaned who was in the greater danger, because they did not give them the right foods. Also, if they did not come to the Clinic they missed the anti-malarial drug. There was a great need to teach public health in this area but it was also very difficult as the people did not wish to change their way of living, because it was what their ancestors taught them. They feared the anger of their spirits if they disobeyed their teaching, and this could result in sickness or even death.

During the time Patsy Russell was with me, we worked together in the Baby Clinic (Kilo) At first the mothers were reluctant to bring their babies to us, being terrified of the vaccinations we were offering them. Measles was a great killer, much more virulent than I had ever seen at home. We had a measles vaccine programme and in all about 3000 children were given the Triple Vaccine against measles, whooping cough and mumps. I do not remember even one adverse reaction after this vaccine was given. Over the years we greatly reduced the number of measles cases which had taken so many lives previously.

We had many mothers coming to the Baby Clinic who were from the Batwa tribe; not true pygmies but had pygmy blood in them. They were not allowed to live in the village with the Bantu folk but had their own settlement on the outskirts of Tondo. When they had their first baby, they came to the clinic dressed in a very bright red 'mini' skirt, and their bodies were covered with a red powder called 'ngola' taken from the camwood tree. They remained dressed like this until the baby was weaned; often two to three years. This was an old ancestral custom.

It was when the baby was weaned that trouble started. Up to then they were very healthy babies but weaning was a rapid introduction to solid food. A date was fixed and a weaning celebration took place which involved a lot of dancing and drinking. Over night, the baby was taken off breast milk and only given solid food. As a result the baby rapidly suffered from diarrhoea and vomiting and quickly lost weight. We tried to educate them into gradual transmission from milk to solids but they were afraid to do this because their ancestors would be angry with them. In most villages we were confronted with severe cases of Kwashiorkor, a very severe malnutrition due to lack of protein in the diet. This occured soon after the child was weaned.

A child of three was brought to us one day suffering from convulsions. The old grandmother had treated her by putting acid drops in her eyes. Both eyes were so badly burnt that the child became totally blind. The following day two children from the same village were brought to us. They were barely conscious and had been suffering from high fevers; probably malaria. The relatives had given them very strong and potent native enemas. Both children died.

Children's Feeding Programme

In 1972 we commenced a Feeding Programme at Tondo, in conjunction with Tear Fund, to feed and treat these children. In some cases the mother had died and the grandparents were bringing the children to us, together with five or six other children. Although there was fish in the lake, this was dried and taken to local markets where it was sold for a great price. In the meantime, their children died.

I had about 60 children regularly on the Feeding Programme. One little lad I will never forget. His mother died in childbirth in their village, due to meddlesome midwifery. The father rushed him over to us by canoe, as the mother's relatives were trying to take the child and kill him, because they said 'the baby killed his mother, therefore we will kill the baby.' He was named Mabala, which was his mother's name, but this is the custom; that whether boy or girl, a baby who loses his or her mother in childbirth, is given the mother's name. I cared for Mabala for 5 years and when the relatives saw what a beautiful child he was, they wanted him back.

During those five years his brothers and sisters also came on to the Feeding Programme. One day, when Mabala was a bit naughty, I threw him some old Christmas cards to look at. Most of them had the Nativity scene on them. He picked out one and brought it to me saying, 'Mama, look, Jesus is not on this card; He's gone to die for us on the cross!' A statement of faith from a five year old!

Over the years the Children's Feeding programme continued to be a very needful part of our work. We had some very pathetic cases amongst the children.

A man called Mola came one day with a little girl called Bakamba, aged about eighteen months. The mother had died. The people in the village told him to feed her an egg a day and she would be alright. We think that the mother's relatives probably put him up to this, hoping that Bakamba would die. Mola, being a little simple, did as they told him. Eventually, one of the Christians in the village persuaded him to bring Bakamba to us, which he did. She weighed just 10 pounds; she couldn't crawl or attempt to stand. With the correct food, she soon made leaps and bounds. When the father had to return to the village, she was quite happy to stay and play with Mabala.

As well as the children, there were also many old people needing help and care. Like the children, many of them were ill through malnutrition, with no means themselves of working for money to buy food. I tried to help them out from my own food stock, but it was very difficult."

Amidst all the busy activities of the Mission, times of relaxation and fun were always slotted into the routine programme. Christmas was no exception. Mary gives us a few insights.

"I was always far too busy at Christmas to be homesick! It was lovely to celebrate the birth of our Lord without all the trappings of commercialism. The Congolese people had their traditions as we do. They didn't exchange gifts, but it was their custom for everyone to have something new to wear on Christmas Day.

As we had 60 children on the Feeding Programme which we ran in conjunction with Tear Fund, and also about 40 needy folk in conjunction with Help the Aged, we had to find new clothes for them all. With thanks at that time for the Baptist Missionary Society who sent out 'Wants Boxes' full of clothes and other needful items for the poor folk, we were able to meet the need. Two days before one Christmas, 4 orphan children turned up, whose parents had died and the grandparents could no longer afford to feed them. I had no more new clothes for them, but as I was nearing furlough, I took down my curtains and made dresses, shirts and shorts for them.

We didn't have turkeys in Congo, but we bought two pigs from the Catholic nuns who ran a farm at Bikoro. One larger one for the Feeding Programme folks and a smaller one for the missionary staff. We kept and fed them well before Christmas. When the time came to prepare them for Christmas, we told two Batwa workmen who were looking after them, to be very careful how they got them out of the shed. That morning, when I was doing a Baby Clinic in the hospital, there was a sudden panic. The two workmen came rushing to the hospital hysterically calling to me.

"Mama, come quickly. Our Christmas dinner is swimming away!"

"What!" I exclaimed. "I thought I warned you to be careful when you let those pigs out of the shed. Where are they now?"

Within minutes the station was alerted and a whirlwind of activity was set into motion. Dr Lewis Mullins was with us on this particular occasion, so he rushed round to find Lyn Collis, and together they got into a canoe and paddled rapidly across the lake. By this time the pigs had covered quite a distance and there was now a crowd of onlookers on the beach.

"Bokenda noki, bokenda noki." (Go, Go quickly.) they shrieked, together with an accompanying 'medley' of high pitched shouts of encouragement!

The men finally overtook the pigs, but then the fun really began. How to steer two struggling pigs into an open canoe in the middle of the lake!

"We'll have to go back and get some strong rope," said Lyn, "and tow them in. No way can we get that lot into the canoe!" So this is what they did, finally reaching the land amidst cheers and shrieks and barking dogs, from the excited audience. That is one Christmas dinner I will never forget!!

Each Christmas I did a Nativity play with the children and the adults always looked forward to it. I remember one Christmas, everything was set and we were about to start. The curtains were being pulled and there was Mary and the Angel Gabriel having a real 'punch up' just outside the church. This was all over a bit of tinsel which they both wanted on their head dresses! I quickly took it, broke it in half and gave them half each! Then they calmly walked on to the stage as if nothing had happened, in a most 'holy' fashion, to play their very important parts in the play!

We had no Christmas trees in Congo, so we made artificial ones. One year I had just finished decorating the tree for the children on the Feeding Programme with a little gift for each child. Mabala, the little child I was fostering, came into the lounge, looked at the tree and burst out crying.

"Mabala," I asked, "What is the matter?"

"Mama, where is Jakai (Zacchaeus)" he replied.

"I'll find him," I said.

Then out of my flannelgraph pictures I found Jakai and sat him on the tree. All tears then dried up. Of course these children were not familiar with Christmas trees. The one important tree in the Bible for them at that age, was the story of Jakai climbing in the tree to see Jesus.

Christmas morning we always went to the hospital and told the Christmas story and gave every patient a gift of soap, sugar and an article of clothing. Christmas afternoon we all had a bathe in the lake, then we went round the whole village with the children, singing carols and joining in their African country dances. In the evening we made a bonfire in the compound. The children sat round and sang carols and enjoyed little pancakes with Golden syrup on them. So a crowd of very sticky hands and faces went to bed that night; sticky, but happy."

As the years passed, Mary became more and more involved in the wide area of villages that surrounded Tondo; an area about the size of Wales. So between her many activities, she sought to minister and help as much as possible, slotting in visits as often as she could, into her busy programme.

Chapter 14

MID TERM HOLIDAYS

My Presence will go with you, and I will give you rest.
Exodus 33v14 (NIV)

With the concentration of work in the tropics, it was necessary to have a break from the routine from time to time. Mary tells us something about the holidays she experienced and the complicated travel arrangements that had to be endured.

"No holiday brochures in Congo! However, we always had a half term break which meant that we could have a month away from our station. But where to go? Usually, we visited another mission station, and it was good to see colleagues who worked many miles from Tondo. I remember one August when the schools were on holiday, and Winnie Hadden was also due for a mid term break. She said one day.

"Mary, how about going to Yuli together?"

I agreed it would be a good idea. This was a Mission station of the Regions Beyond Missionary Union, and was where Dr James and Peggy Burton had started their missionary career, before coming to Tondo. They had built and developed a hospital from a small dispensary, back in 1949. Yuli was a village, about the same size as Tondo, in the Basankusu area, north east of Mbandaka. We contacted the folks at Yuli and they said they would be delighted to see new faces. So the trip was arranged.

The first part of the journey involved a 100 kilometre trip from Tondo to Mbandaka in the Tondo Land Rover with a Congolese chauffer. The time it would take to reach our destination depended on the state of the road. After a rainstorm it could be very difficult and the vehicle would slip and slide on the wet, sandy soil. Also the planks on many bridges along the dykes were often rotting and very slippery. If we slipped we would descend into a watery ditch, and this would involve many hours delay. Which side of the road you travelled on depended on any large holes in the road. This was difficult when faced with any oncoming traffic!

As we passed one spot, I remembered that a few weeks previously, a large lorry had taken the bend in the road too fast, and had overturned. It had been loaded with drums of petrol, paraffin oil, palm oil, large bunches of bananas and plantains and kwanga (manioc) On top of all this there were many passengers, including women and children. Sadly, some of the passengers were killed and many were injured. The driver escaped unhurt and ran into the forest for his life, before the passengers who were unhurt, beat him up!

We passed small villages on the way as we travelled on, where crowds of children, sheep goats and chickens would run on to the road. But the people welcomed us and gave us gifts of chickens, eggs and fruit.

On arrival at Mbandaka, we went to the American Mission of the Disciples of Christ, situated on the shores of the great Congo River and stayed there the night. It was lovely to enjoy American hospitality and good to taste cheese, fresh meat and apples, which were not available at Tondo.

The next day we boarded a small boat to take us up the river on the way to Yuli. We literally fought our way on to the boat with the help of a Congolese porter who carried our suitcases on his head. There were crowds of people either trying to board the boat or alight from it, with much shouting, screaming and pushing. Mothers were carrying small babies on their backs and luggage on their heads. All of us scrambled up a narrow plank which acted as a gangway.

River Boat

This was one of the smaller river passenger boats which had a small deck on top with two or three first class cabins, then on the deck below, were the second class cabins. Here there was much noise and shouting. The third class was on the lower deck, where there were no cabins at all. Here the folks were fighting to acquire a convenient place to sleep between the cargo. This area also served as a boat market.

Our cabin was very small, hot and humid. We stowed our luggage below the bunks, and paid the porter who had done a really good job in getting us safely on board. Then we leant over the railings on the deck and watched with interest the confusion going on as people struggled to get all their belongings on board.

Eventually, the sirens sounded and the boarding plank was hauled up. The engines came into life and we slowly left our moorings. As we chugged up the river it got narrower and narrower as we entered the great Congo forest. There was plenty of activity to watch on the decks below. Traders were spreading their wares on the deck floor, selling cheap jewellery, second hand clothing, palm oil, hurricane lamps, spare wicks and lamp globes together with many other goods. Sadly, we saw medicines being sold without any advice as to how they should be administered. Antibiotics were being sold in ones and twos. I just longed to tell the folks that less than 20 capsules could do more harm than good. There was much noise as everyone was trying to bargain, hoping to reduce the price of the vendor.

Babies were being bathed in a large bowl filled with river water. Then, to add to the confusion, chickens, ducks and goats were loudly letting their presence be known. The scenery on either side of the boat was of dense forest trees. We saw monkeys swaying and jumping from branch to branch and beautiful birds, such as kingfishers, herons, hornbills and parrots. Occasionally we noticed a crocodile or a hippopotamus.

Then we would come to a clearing in the forest where there would be a small village. The plank was put in place, a rope thrown to a man on the shore, who then tied it to a tree. Immediately the villagers tried to board the boat, selling fish, chickens, monkeys, vegetables and fruit of all kinds. Some of them in their hurry fell off the plank with the loss of their wares! Then small boys would dive into the water to retrieve as much as possible and to receive a reward from the owner. The hubbub was terrific and it made a very colourful scene, as everyone seemed to be happy. New passengers had to fight their way on to the boat, as others were trying to leave at the same time. Eventually, the sirens sounded, the engines started and the rope was untied from the tree and thrown aboard as we slowly moved on. Some unfortunate passengers did not get off in time so would have to wait for the next village and hope to find a friend with a canoe to take them back.

During the evening hours when things quietened down, we would venture on to the decks below and talk to the folks, sharing with them the Good News of Jesus and giving them Bibles, hymn books and tracts. We met several Congolese Christians who worked with us. If we were travelling on a Sunday, we obtained permission from the Captain to hold a Service on the decks. We were never refused, so we were able to make Jesus known amongst these people, many of whom were living in constant fear of evil spirits.

River boats did not travel at night but stopped to load on wood for the engines. Sleep at night was almost impossible as the logs were continually thrown on to the decks until the early hours. Then the deck hands started to scrub the decks, singing lively African songs at the same time.

We eventually arrived at our destination. Here we were met by the Yuli mission truck driven by a very pleasant Congolese chauffer, who assisted us off the boat with our luggage. So we started along the rough road to Yuli. By evening, just before sunset, the chauffer said we could not go any further that night. We were a long way from the next village.

"Why?" we asked.

"Don't you see those droppings on the road?" he replied. "They are elephant droppings and it is not safe to continue."

So we resigned ourselves to the fact that the three of us would have to spend the night in the cabin of the truck. Next morning, with the very beautiful sight of the dawn breaking through the trees, we recommenced our journey. With the morning chorus of the birds, we just praised God for His wonderful creation.

As we drove into Yuli village, there was a large crowd to greet us and a special welcome from Elsie Saunders, the senior missionary there. We spent two very happy weeks with her, and made friends with many of the Congolese folks. Fortunately, we spoke Lingala, the trade language, so we were able to communicate with the people.

On our journey back to Tondo, we were not met by elephants this time, and the boat journey was the same; equally noisy and interesting. The road from Mbandaka to Tondo was not so wet or slippery. So we returned to Tondo refreshed both physically and spiritually to continue the work God had called us to do.

At other times we would spend our mid term break in the capital, Kinshasa, formally called Leopoldville. This holiday served two purposes, to give us a holiday in a lovely city providing all modern facilities, and also to do a great deal of shopping to replenish our stocks at Tondo. We usually chose to travel by river boat enjoying the picturesque and interesting scenery en route.

These large boats travelled regularly from Kisangani in the north, to Kinshasa, the capital, in the south, stopping at Government posts and large villages on the way. The first class passengers were given cabins, and there was a dining room on board. The cook was very friendly and we were able to fill our thermos flasks with boiling water to enable us to make tea and coffee in our cabins. We always travelled with a supply of instant coffee, tea bags and powered milk.

The second class accommodation was the same as on the smaller boats but of course much larger; therefore more colourful and noisy! These larger boats did not travel by night because of the danger of being stuck on a sandbank. As we travelled down river, it was good to stop at the Baptist Missionary Stations, Bolobo and Lukolela, where we had time to go ashore and meet our colleagues there. As these boats were so much bigger than the one we travelled on to Yuli, they had to moor quite a distance from the shore. This meant that four men had to dive into the muddy water with a steel cable which they would fasten to a large tree. This was also repeated at the stern of the boat. Then a gangway was lowered with two planks. Immediately, dozens of canoes would surround the boat, some to collect passengers; some to take new passengers on board. Then the bedlam of many traders fighting their way on board to sell their wares. It was fascinating to watch, despite the noise, and interesting to notice the comradeship and cheerfulness amongst the Congolese.

So as the gangway and steel cables were drawn back into the boat, we continued on our way to Kinshasa to be met by our missionaries colleagues there. Having come from the forest area into a much more modern and sophisticated environment, we felt very much like the 'country cousins.' We enjoyed sharing news with the folks there and enjoyed the modern facilities of this 'city holiday,' and a visit to the large market with its selection of coloured cloth, food and goods of every kind."

The two holidays described here happened before Independence. After 1960 it was not safe for Europeans to travel so freely, and a mid term break would be greatly reduced. However, Mary would never forget these wonderful times as she looked back over the years.

———————

Chapter 15

SERVING THE LORD IN THE CONGOLESE CHURCH

Jesus went through all the towns and villages, teaching in their
synagogues, preaching the good news of the Kingdom and healing
every disease and sickness.
Matthew 9v35 (NIV)

Quite a bit of Mary's ministry was involved in church responsibilities, both on the Mission and in the villages. She also spent a lot of time amongst the Batwa people. In the district around Tondo, she came into contact with a lot of witchcraft. Here are some of her reports about her church commitments at Tondo and in the surrounding district.

"Congo was originally a Belgian Colony. Therefore in the small villages there were both Roman Catholic and Protestant churches. Before Christianity was brought to the Congo, the people were animists, believing in the spirit world, and a supreme being who controlled their lives. There were also witch doctors throughout the land and faith in their fetishes made from bird's claws, feathers, teeth, horn or human hair, was very strong. These witch doctors also prescribed native medicine, often produced from the right source, but given in strong, lethal doses. Faith in these medicine men was strong , especially as it was tied up with belief in the spirits of their ancestors. This all made the medical work very difficult for European doctors and nurses. Even some Congolese Christians found it difficult to discard their faith in these witch doctors completely, and in times of severe distress, would turn back to them again.

We had one patient brought into the hospital one day. The relatives were sure he was going to die because they had put a curse on him. They even brought the coffin to the hospital. This man was a Christian, and we prayed for him claiming the victory over Satan. We operated on him for a strangulated hernia and he made a good recovery. Another witness to God's power over the work of the devil. We set fire to the empty coffin.

In each village we visited we would do church work as well as medical. We found that many church members had been put out of fellowship because they had gone into polygamous marriage, or were living in adultery. They were welcomed to the church services but until they sorted things out, were not allowed to take part in the Communion Service. Polygamy rules were very difficult for the new Christian to accept, as polygamy was not frowned upon in animistic beliefs. Others were removed from the church membership because they made or sold palm wine, which was a very strong drink. One man was brought into the hospital seemingly unconscious, but we discovered that he had drunk many glasses of this wine. It was three days before he came round.

Evangelism was not very popular amongst the Batwa people. The pygmies in our area were originally a very despised tribe. Years ago they were slaves to the Bantu and each pygmy family was owned by a Bantu family. They were not allowed to live in the village with the Bantu, but had their own encampment outside the main village. They were not allowed to eat or marry with the Bantu people, and even while I was at Tondo they would have to ask permission from the descendants of the family who originally owned them, to marry. We therefore felt there was a great need to work amongst them, as a witness, not only to them, but also to the Bantu, to teach them all, that in God's sight we are equally precious to him.

Much to the disgust of the Bantu, I took on a Batwa lad as my houseboy. I found that he was the most reliable and honest of all the houseboys who had worked for me. My Congolese friends thought that I was in mortal danger because I ate the food he prepared for me!

We had a Sunday School for the Batwa folk and not only the children came, but many of the adults too. We built a little chapel in their compound and gradually they responded to the Good News of Jesus Christ. We also discovered that they had beautiful singing voices and soon formed their own choir. Much to our delight the Congolese eventually accepted them in the main church, delighted by their singing.

Nsaka was a particularly keen Batwa man and wanted to learn as much as he could. We took him as a worker in the hospital and taught him how to use our sterilizer; similar to a pressure cooker. One day I wanted some sterilizing to be done in an emergency and couldn't find the sterilizer anywhere. I eventually found it in Nsaka's house; his wife was cooking her fish in it! At the time, Nsaka had been busy doing the hospital laundry in the lake and didn't know that the sterilizer had disappeared! We were so pleased with Nsaka's work that when his little hut virtually fell down, we built him a new house made with sun dried brick. After it was finished, he refused to move into it. He said that the evil spirits had taken possession of it. We called our Pastor and church elders and together we went to his new house and prayed in every room against the evil spirits. After that, Nsaka lived very happily and peacefully in his new house.

Eventually, as time went by, the brightest lads were accepted in the school, and when I eventually retired, it was wonderful to see the first ordained Batwa Pastor leading his own flock. With God all things are possible.

En route to village clinic

We tried to do more for the Batwa folks who tend to be rejected by the other tribes. The State is trying to upgrade them into the life of the people. In their camps I held Baby Clinics, because they just wouldn't come to the regular one Ikoma had in the hospital. Given the opportunity of education, they were just as intelligent as any other race. There were some very lovable and loyal folks among them and many of them were my friends.

I remember the wife of one of our workmen was brought into the hospital one evening, having gone into the forest to collect firewood to cook the evening meal. A strong storm suddenly blew up and a huge branch of a tree fell on top of her, splitting her scalp. Fortunately, the bone wasn't fractured. She was unconscious for about a week, then gradually came round. Her wounds healed very well, but mentally she was very slow and sluggish and we doubted that she would ever return to be quite normal again. But on the whole, our work amongst the Batwa people went well and we pray that many of these little folks may come to a saving knowledge of the Lord.

We discovered one Batwa family at Nzalakenga, about 32 kilometres away from the Mission. The mother was lying in her little mud hut and her blood count registered at only 20%. Her body was full of oedema and obviously she had a heart condition as well. She had a baby with her of about 9 months, grossly undernourished, also another child of two years old. The father made no efforts to get medical help so we arranged for our hospital workmen with a stretcher, to bring her and the family back to the hospital. The baby progressed well, but the mother was very ill, her life expectancy very limited.

Another rather neglected work in the church was amongst the youth. With the help of the missionary school teachers in the Sunday School, some of the Congolese teachers were trained in youth work, and a thriving Sunday School for 5 – 11 year olds was established.

The Mission church grew and developed over the years. Each year we had special services for Christmas, Easter and a Harvest Festival, when the church was decorated with greenery. The people brought their offerings of fruit and vegetables and also live stock. One harvest service was livened by a particular rooster who decided that he had had enough and started crowing at the top of his voice. One lad took the initiative and chased the rooster round the church. Eventually, he plopped a basket over it and then sat on the basket until the end of the service!

Easter morning dawned with a happy band of Christians singing hymns of praise as at 6am they wended their way down to the lakeside to witness the ordinance of Baptist. On this occasion, four of our senior school lads were baptised together with two old leprosy patients. Their faces truly shone forth the love of the Lord as they came out of the water. What great riches they had received in accepting Jesus as their Lord and Saviour.

I'll always remember on a particular Sunday morning service when a Congolese Pastor was preaching. At one point a very large cockroach was climbing up the front of the pulpit and was just about to walk over his Bible and notes. He hastily called the folks to pray, and when the eyes of the faithful were closed, he flicked the menacing insect off the pulpit with his finger and it landed on the front pew! Happily, true to Baptist tradition, nobody was sitting in the front pew. I wonder whose eyes were open!

During another service a sudden storm blew up. It thundered and the lightning was terrifying. It struck the Pastor's wife and she fell to the ground unconscious. We all thought she had died. Many heartfelt SOS prayers were made and to our utter relief she gradually came round. It was a great witness to all those present as it was a miracle that she recovered. It reminded me of the day when I was visiting in the village. On entering Mpembe's little mud hut I said to her, "Mbote Mama, how are you keeping?" She replied, "Mama, I'm not keeping, I'm being kept." So we have proved many times in Congo, His hand has always been upon us, especially in very difficult circumstances.

We do a lot of work amongst the women at Tondo, and each Tuesday afternoon we had a Women's Worship Service. As a result of these meetings a group of women would go to the outlying villages each weekend to take services themselves. It often meant a trek of 32 kilometres to reach their destination. The Congolese are born actors, so the Scriptures were taught by putting on plays at Tondo and elsewhere. We had great fun together rehearsing and organising these plays. We also taught the women some sewing skills, and some even mastered the use of a sewing machine.

In every village we visited we found more and more cases of kwashiorkor, a protein deficiency disease. Also there were many cases of hunger and resulting malnutrition in families where there were five or more children. The folks just could not afford to buy fish which was their main source of protein food. Also, the fish harvest from the lake was sometimes very poor. One of the reasons for starting the Feeding Programme was because of these conditions that we were finding.

One day I was doing a clinic in the open air under a large mango tree in a village across the lake called Nkake. I noticed a little Batwa women standing on the edge of the crowd. Batwa folk are despised by the other folks, and unless we called them to the front, they would be made to wait until last. I called her to me and saw what I thought was a bone protruding out from her left cheek. On examination I discovered that it was a rotten tooth. She had a huge hole in her cheek. This was the first time I had extracted a tooth through the side of a person's face! We brought her back to the hospital and removed seven decayed teeth. She was also very anaemic and suffering from malnutrition. What did we do about the hole in her face? We could not send her to Kinshasa for plastic surgery, so we just improved her general condition and at least gave her a clean mouth and sent her back to her village. A pathetic old lady and our hearts went out to her, but at least we know that we did all that was possible for her, and when she left us she was quite happy and was feeling so much better.

To walk round a typical village at 7am, you would find very few folks around. The women would be off to their gardens with a large basket on their back in which there would be a machete, hoe and a bottle of drinking water. Some of the women would have a baby secured on their chests or riding on their shoulders. The gardens were often as much as 4 kilometres away from the village.

When I was in a particular village one Tuesday, I usually did a Baby Clinic (known as Kilo, because we weighed the babies each week) This was always held on a Tuesday because the women said that they would never go to their gardens on a Tuesday because that was the day the evil spirits would be there. One week our Pastor's wife, Elisa, said,

"I'm going to my garden this Tuesday; I'm a Christian and am not afraid of evil spirits." The other women were horrified. But off she went. Later that morning Mama Elisa came running back; she looked terrified. I asked her.

"Mama Elisa, what is the matter?"

"I went to my garden," she replied, "and while I was working a large black thing came out of the forest, put its arms round my neck and tried to strangle me. I said to him, 'I belong to Jesus and you can't hurt me', and I repeated the name, Jesus, Jesus, and at the name of Jesus, the evil spirit fled back into the forest.". Later, several other Christians told me that they too had had similar experiences.

Early in the morning the men folk would be off in their canoes fishing or off to the forest with their dogs to hunt; they too would not go hunting in the forest on a Tuesday.

Many of the old folks would be mostly sitting in the village 'meeting house'. This was a shelter covered with an ndele (palm leaf) roof, no walls, but a wooden bench either side, and a wood fire burning in the middle, to keep the mosquitoes at bay. They would probably be smoking their clay pipes. This was a good opportunity to share our faith with them.

The men folk usually arrived back to the village about 3pm. The women would be preparing the evening meal for the family. All the little camp fires would be brightly burning outside each house. If the fishermen had a successful day, they might give the smaller fish to their wives to cook, but most of the fish was dried and sold at the markets. All the meat which was hunted would be sold and not eaten in the village unless a Chief was visiting. There was a taboo against red meat and eggs. They would not drink goat's milk, and when they discovered that our powdered milk originated from a cow, they refused that too.

On moonlight nights after the meal, there would be dancing and singing, often right through the night.

Saturday afternoon was always 'hair dressing day'. Walking round the village you would see young girls and women seated in pairs, making the most elaborate hair styles; tiny plaits tied round tightly with black cotton. On returning from furlough I always had to bring a good supply of black cotton reels with me.

Talking drum

On Sunday the morning service would be heralded by a drum calling the people to worship. The service could be as long as two to three hours in length, with plenty of singing and an offering that could take as long as half an hour. The women would give their gifts first, dancing up the aisle with them, then the men would give theirs. There was always rivalry to see who would give the most. Usually the women did best!

Of course the normal routine of the village was interrupted from time to time by funerals or sickness. Weddings were rare in the villages as most of them would go to the nearest State Post where the girl's name would be put into the husband's State Identification book. Then they would be considered legally married.

Funerals always took place as soon as possible after death, because of the very hot and humid climate. There would be much wailing, an expression of their grief and the appeasement of the evil spirits. They could never understand why we were silent when we received news of a loved one passing. A Christian funeral however, would be much quieter and reverent. Although after the burial, there would inevitably be a certain amount of wailing. This did help them to overcome their grief.

It was lovely to travel across Lake Tumba by canoe to visit the villages on the far shore. Ikoko Bonginda was a favourite spot about 20 kilometres away. If petrol was available, we would attach an outboard motor at the back of the canoe, otherwise we would take some Congolese men with us and paddle across. This took much longer and could be dangerous if we were caught suddenly by a storm. Like the Sea of Galilee, a storm could blow up quite unexpectedly. This would mean 'all hands on deck' as the waves could be quite big. The paddlers would turn the canoe to face the waves and not alongside them, as this would probably turn the canoe over. They would paddle as hard as they could heading for the nearest shore. All the time we would bail out the water with a small scoop, and be praying! Sometimes we would have to spend the night in a small nearby village. However, on a calm and lovely sunny day, it was very relaxing to travel in a canoe across the lake.

Some of our Congolese friends could predict the weather. I remember one day when we were all ready to make a journey across the lake, the canoe was packed; the lake was like a mill pond. It seemed an ideal time to set off but we were told, 'No, you can't go yet.' 'Why not?' we asked. 'Because, look round the lake. Can you see that palm tree leaf just waving in the breeze? That means that in the direction we are going, a storm will soon blow up.' So we waited until the next day before we could leave, and their prediction proved right!

After I returned from one of our lake trips however, I felt very unwell for about a month; very lethargic, loss of appetite and all my bones seemed to ache. Then one day when I had gone to another village to do medical work, I laid down on the camp bed after a midday snack and dozed off for a short while. When I woke up I felt completely different. I had my old energy back and no aches and pains. The tummy ache and sick feeling had completely disappeared, and from then on I was fine. I am sure that someone at home must have been praying for me, because it was such a sudden change. How faithful is the One who has called me to serve in Congo.

On all our journeys we were always very assured of God's hand upon us. His promises proved true 'The Lord shall preserve thy going out and thy coming in from this time forth, and even for ever more.' Psalm 121v8"

So in all her experiences Mary relied entirely on the strength of the God she had come to Congo to serve. She loved the people and wanted to do all that she could to relieve their suffering, but above all, to point them to the one and true God. He alone could lead them into the way of truth and free them from all their fears and doubts. God was continually at work amongst the people of Congo, and He relied upon us all to radiate His love and care.

Chapter 16

UP AND AWAY

The time has come for my departure.
2Timothy 4v6

"When I first came to the Belgian Congo in 1954, I came as a long term missionary, and I knew that I would not return to the UK for good until such time as the Lord called me to do so, even if it meant staying on after the normal age of retirement. However, the call to return to the UK came in December 1983, the morning when Angus McNeil, our Field Secretary, was due to be in Tondo interviewing missionaries. The Word from God given me that very morning in my Quiet Time was 'Up! Go away! This is no more your land and home.' Then later, when I was talking with Angus he asked me when I was planning to go home on furlough to retire, and advised me that in view of Rosemary Giboney already having been assigned to Tondo to replace me, it would be expedient that I return without too long an overlap with her. If I stayed on in Tondo, Rosemary would be sent to another of our BMS stations where they were very short of nurses, and this would leave Wilma Aitchison on her own. I was planning myself, to return home in June 1984.

I knew that BMS were not happy for missionaries, especially single ones, to stay on after retirement age, as they feared that as we grow older we would be a burden on younger missionaries! I insisted on spending Christmas 1983 in Tondo, as this would be the last time I could ever spend a Christmas in Congo. So plans were made for me to return to the UK in January 1984, and I certainly wasn't looking forward to the cold of January, leaving temperatures of 90-100 degrees!

The last few weeks in Tondo were very busy indeed. Although we had no doctor in the hospital at that time, we did have a very efficient Congolese staff. Our senior nurse, Ikoma Denis, had been trained by Dr James Burton to operate, and he was now operating regularly, doing hernia repairs, appendectomy, caesarean sections and other major operations successfully. The people had great confidence in him, and so did we.

Wilma and I were concentrating on Public Health work. We had opened four Health Centres, three in villages across the lake and one inland. The State had given us a new refrigerator to keep vaccines, and also they sent us a specially trained nurse in vaccination. He regularly visited all these Health Centres. TB vaccines were given to all under 14 year olds, as TB was very wide spread. We had virtually controlled measles in the area, which up to now had been a real killer amongst the under five year olds. All together, in public health and the hospital work, we were employing sixty nursing staff, all the Public Health nurses' salaries being paid for by the State.

At Tondo itself, we were very busy working in conjunction with Help the Aged and Tear Fund, treating the very malnourished children and destitute elderly folk who had been abandoned by their relatives. With monies sent out by Help the Aged, we were able to build six houses for them, and repair many other houses. We gave them a hot meal each day, soap and paraffin oil for their lamps when it was available. One of the elderly ladies, Mboyo, had two mentally deficient sons who were a real menace in the village. We housed Mboyo to protect her as relatives were saying an evil spirit in her, caused her sons mental condition. There was also another old couple who were notoriously very difficult and had antagonised all their relatives, so were abandoned and were sent to us to care for them. Some of our deacons who were watching us work one day said to me,

"Mama, now we know what the love of God means."

With the help of Steve Mantle, a BMS missionary, several wells had been dug in Tondo and other villages, providing good drinking water. The dry season had been exceptionally dry and all the water sources in Tondo dried up. We had been going by canoe across the lake to get water from springs there. Steve's wife, Isabel, was also a nurse so was able to help us in the hospital. Through our medical and church work, the Gospel of Jesus Christ was being proclaimed.

During my last few days at Tondo, the folks were coming to my door asking to be given, or buy my belongings. One man even begged me to give him my false teeth!

Then after many farewell meals, the day came when I had to leave Tondo. As we drove out of the village I saw the little lad, Mabala, who I had fostered for so many years, crying his eyes out. That broke my heart and I just couldn't keep the tears back.

I don't think I really got excited about going home until I took off in the plane from Kinshasa airport. Both my parents had passed away, and were with our Lord in Glory. The family home was occupied by Campus Crusade missionaries, so for the first six months I lived with my 90 year old Aunt. I really enjoyed those first few months with her, and we had great times of fellowship together. I shall always thank the Lord for giving me two such good brothers and sister-in-laws, who made my father change his will and leave the family home to me. As they said, 'We have our homes and Mary will have nowhere to live when she comes home.' I was able to sell the house and bought a bungalow in Southwick to be near my younger brother and sister-in-law, Norah. I wanted my Aunt to come and live with me, but sadly, not long before the move, she went to be with the Lord. Sad for me, but a happy homecoming for her.

So the move to Southwick in Sussex. The day before I moved, all the furniture I possessed was a bed, coffee table from Congo and a bureau. The furniture from the old home was far too big. The evening before, my nephew Colin, had hired a small van to take my bits and pieces. That evening I had several phone calls. 'Can you do with some dining room furniture? Our son is putting it on the tip as they are going in for antique furniture.' Another said, 'Do you need bedroom furniture?' And so it went on. Next day my home was fully furnished. God is no one's debtor!

———

EPILOGUE

During the first six months at home I was fully engaged with Home Assignments for the Baptist Missionary Society. I thoroughly enjoyed this experience, and made many new friends, and have kept in touch with them. Apart from Northern Ireland, I saw most of Great Britain! This meant that I was away most weekends, and although Holland Road Baptist Church in Hove, gave me a wonderful 'Welcome Home,' it was a few more months before I could worship there regularly.

I officially retired at the end of June 1984, and then was free to become involved in the church work at Holland Road. I enjoyed teaching in the Sunday School (Discoverers), and then when I was a little older – and a little deaf – I left Discoverers and was asked to take over the leadership of the Tuesday afternoon service, which is specifically for the older generation who cannot make it to church on Sunday evenings. As several of these ladies and gentlemen are also a little deaf, we understand each other very well! I also enjoy being involved in a House group, and helping on Friday mornings with our Friendship Centre when we serve a lunch for anyone who likes to drop in. This too, is very enjoyable, and we have good fellowship and fun together.

Also during my retirement I completed my studies with the Christian Training Programme of the Baptist Union of Great Britain. In 1993 I received their Lay Preacher's Certificate and Diploma. In 1990 I became President of the Sussex Baptist Women's Association and the Sussex Baptist Association. in 1995.

Congo is now officially known as the Democratic Republic of Congo. (DRC) It is a vast country consisting of many different tribes, each with their own language and customs. There has been much unrest, and inevitable wars as so many factions lust for overall power. This has resulted in much suffering, especially in the north east of Congo. The economy has suffered and many of the public services have broken down. There is wide spread poverty, and HIV and AIDS has left an estimated two million orphans in the country. For many in the DRC, education is a luxury, and school personnel have gone for long periods without any pay.

Much prayer is needed for this beautiful country. We praise the Lord that His church is strong and vibrant, and the Congolese Christians face the future with much courage and faith.

I do thank and praise our Lord for all His faithful care and protection during my years in Congo. I pray that this book may be an inspiration to young folks, and also not so young, to serve Him wherever He leads. Jesus said,

"All authority in heaven and on earth has been given to Me. Therefore go and makedisciples of all nations, ...And surely I am with you always, to the very end of the age."
Matthew 28v18-20

GLOSSARY

Belgian Congo	
Zaire	Democratic Republic of Congo
Leopoldville	Kinshasa – Capital
Stanleyville	Kisangani
Coquilhatville	Mbandaka
BMS	Baptist Missionary Society
ECHO	Equipment for Charity Hospitals Overseas
DCCM	Disciples of Christ Congo Mission
ABFMS	American Baptist Foreign Missionary Society
IME	Institute Medical Evangelique
IRSAC	Belgian Scientific Research Centre
Furlough	Home Assignment.

OTHER BOOKS BY PEGGY BURTON

Mwanza
Flying Forceps
Cheaper by the Million
Lifeline to Millions
Children's Bible story painting books
Challenged to Conquer (autobiography)
Born to Serve (autobiography)
Tales from the Congo Forest
Daily Walks in the Forest

KING'S HIGHWAY SERIES
Commandments for Travellers
Promises for Travellers
Search the Scriptures
Led by the Shepherd
Follow the Shepherd
Great Prayers of the Bible
Great Commandments of the Bible
Great Promises of the Bible

———————————

OTHER BOOKS BY PEGGY BURTON

Mwanza
Flying Forceps
Cheaper by the Million
Lifeline to Millions
Children's Bible story painting books
Challenged to Conquer (autobiography)
Born to Serve (autobiography)
Tales from the Congo Forest
Daily Walks in the Forest

KING'S HIGHWAY SERIES
Commandments for Travellers
Promises for Travellers
Search the Scriptures
Led by the Shepherd
Follow the Shepherd
Great Prayers of the Bible
Great Commandments of the Bible
Great Promises of the Bible

GLOSSARY

Belgian Congo
Zaire   Democratic Republic of Congo

Leopoldville   Kinshasa – Capital
Stanleyville   Kisangani
Coquilhatville Mbandaka

BMS   Baptist Missionary Society
ECHO   Equipment for Charity Hospitals Overseas
DCCM   Disciples of Christ Congo Mission
ABFMS   American Baptist Foreign
       Missionary Society
IME   Institute Medical Evangelique
IRSAC   Belgian Scientific Research Centre
Furlough   Home Assignment.